THE REMEMBERING

A JOURNEY BACK TO SELF

PETER KENNEDY

The Remembering

© 2025, Peter Kennedy

First Edition

Published by Peter Kennedy

www.EvolveWeird.com

Printed in the United States of America

Hardcover ISBN: 979-8-9928672-4-4

Softcover (Paperback) ISBN: 979-8-9928672-9-9

eBook ISBN: 979-8-9928672-8-2

Cover designed by Peter Kennedy

Edited by Taylor Plimpton and Liz Kazandzhy

This is a work of nonfiction. The experiences and lessons shared are based on the author's personal journey. Any references to individuals or events are either factual or used in a transformative way.

To my wife and soulmate, Brooks, who always believed in me. And to my children—Henry, Jackson, Wells, Chloe, and Lily—whom I love dearly.

CONTENTS

Preface   xiii

1. THE MOMENT OF SURRENDER   1
    The Heat of Fear   2
    Breaking Past the Threshold   3
    The Test of Surrender   4
    The Vision   6
    Emerging Reborn   9
    The Shaman's Message   12
    The Awakening   17

2. THE ILLUSION OF ENOUGH   21
    My Father—Discipline as a Way of Life   21
    The Pull of Instant Gratification   23
    The Quiet Force of a Mother's Love   24
    The Legacy of Greatness   26
    Chasing a Giant   28
    The Mirage of Success   29
    The Fear Equation   30

3. THE PRISON OF BECOMING   33
    The Paradox of Seeking   34
    Trapped in the Loop   35
    Confronting the Voices   35
    The Impossible Chase   36

4. THE SACRED AGREEMENT   37
    The Moment That Changed Everything   38
    A Sacred Contract   39
    The Dharma of Relationships   40
    The Real Work of Love   41
    The Mirror of Love   42

5. THE WAR WITHIN — 45

The Universe Intervenes — 45

Meeting Michelle — 46

Holding a Balloon Underwater — 47

The Man Arrives — 47

The Protector and the Fear of Failure — 48

Enter The Exile — 50

A Life Labeled Before It Even Began — 51

The Teacher's Regret — 52

Meeting Him with Love — 53

The Man Returns — 53

The Battle Begins — 54

6. THE ILLUSION OF DETACHMENT — 55

Chasing Enlightenment Like Success — 55

The Retreats—Searching Beyond Myself — 56

The Illusion of Detachment — 57

7. THE BODY REMEMBERS — 59

The Body Remembers What the Mind Forgets — 60

The Power of Ownership — 60

The Power of Language — 61

The Return of The Man — 62

The Shift That Changed Everything — 62

The Truth I Didn't Want to Hear — 64

8. THE MAN, THE BOY, AND ME — 65

Preparing for the Ceremony — 66

Entering the Ceremony — 66

The Return of The Man — 69

The Purge — 69

The Scream of a Lifetime — 70

The Reunion — 72

The Final Test — 73

9. THE HAMSTER WHEEL — 75

Taking Ownership — 77

Breaking Free—Choosing Awareness Over Blame — 80

10. THE COST OF THE CHASE 81
   The Dream That Started It All 82
   The Pivot 83
   The Turning Point 85
   The Deep Dive 87
   The Moment of Truth 88
   Scaling Beyond the Startup Phase 89
   The Road to Global Expansion 91
   Expanding the Empire 93
   The São Paulo Lesson 95
   Brazilian Business Culture 96
   The Relentless Grind 97
   Hustle at All Costs 98
   The Identity Paradox 100
   Integration, Not Elimination 102
   Fueling the Machine 102

11. THE SALE 109
   The Waiting Game 110
   Paradox of Attachment 111
   The Meeting 113
   The Closing Pitch 116
   The Term Sheet 116
   Drowning in Due Diligence 118
   The Deal That Wouldn't Die 120
   August 3, 2023 121

12. BEYOND THE FINISH LINE 123
   The Moment It Sank In 124
   The Morning After 126
   Rod and the Breaking Point 128

13. THE DISCIPLINE OF AWAKENING 131
   Illusion of Wanting vs. the Reality of Commitment ... 133
   The Power of Daily Practice 134
   A Mirror to My Own Awareness 136
   What You Focus On Grows 136
   A Meeting with My Soul 139
   Into the Void 141
   The Truth in the Void 143

14. FREE . . . BUT NOT FOR LONG   147

   Breaking Through, Breaking Free   147

   The Agreement   150

   The Offer I Never Wanted   152

   A Challenge I Didn't Want to Win   154

   The Space Between What Was and What's Next   156

15. THE CAVE   159

   The Unexpected Influence   160

   The Universe Has Other Plans   161

   Arrival in Oregon   161

   The Last Stop Before Darkness   162

   The Ascent to Sky Cave   163

   Inside the Retreat   165

   Time Stretches   167

   Lost in the Dark   169

   Running Toward Fear, Searching for Proof   170

   Letting Go   172

   Redefining Strength   173

16. EVOLVEWELL   177

   Ikigai—The Intersection of Purpose   178

   The Birth of EvolveWell   179

   The Rare Bird   180

   The Breath That Changed Everything   181

   Learning to Breathe   182

   When the Right People Show Up   184

   The Universe Has Its Own Timing   185

   Personal Growth Before Profits   186

   A Space for Deep Connection   187

   Breathing New Life into Business   188

17. BECOMING THE PRACTICE   191

   My Practice   191

   Finding Your Path   193

   Start Here   194

18. THE CHOICE   197

   Standing Before Source   198

   The Cost of Awakening   199

The Truth   200
Taking Inventory   201
Your Time Is Now   203

Afterword   205
About the Author   207

"The way is not really a way. It is a depth.
It is not a distance.
It is a deepening into the stillness,
stabilizing in the unmoving.
It is not a walking journey.
Journeys are for the body and the ego-mind.
But the subtlety of intuitive seeing takes you deeper
into the bliss of the unknowable."
—Mooji

PREFACE

Transformation is never linear. It doesn't follow a predictable path, nor does it arrive in the way we expect. We like to think growth happens in a straight line—from struggle to breakthrough, from challenge to clarity —but the truth is far messier. It's unpredictable, uncomfortable, and often filled with strange synchronicities that make no sense until we look back. The moments that change us most are rarely the ones we see coming.

At my company, EvolveWell, we have a name for this phenomenon —Evolve Weird—because transformation never unfolds the way we think it will. Life has a way of rerouting us, of delivering lessons in ways that defy logic, of opening doors at the exact right moment—even if we don't understand why. You don't always get what you want, but if you pay attention, you'll realize you always get exactly what you need to evolve.

This book is about that process.

It's about the strange, beautiful, sometimes brutal journey of remembering the parts of yourself you lost, buried, or forgot—and reclaiming the life you were always meant to live.

It's my story—every breakthrough, every misstep, every uncomfortable truth that shaped my path. Some lessons came through deep reflection. Others through relentless trial and error. Many forced me to face fears I'd spent a lifetime avoiding.

This book isn't the end result of transformation.

It's part of the transformation.

And if it meets you at just the right time, maybe it will become part of yours too.

1

THE MOMENT OF SURRENDER

"Your pain is the breaking of the shell that encloses your understanding."
—Khalil Gibran

The temazcal swallowed me whole. The air was thick, suffocating. My skin burned, breath shallow, sweat pouring in waves. Somewhere in the darkness, a drum pounded like a heartbeat, the shaman's voice rising and falling in hypnotic chants. I wanted out. But there was no way out—not yet.

There are moments in life when you know everything is about to change. Our greatest transformations happen when we are stretched beyond our limits. In those moments, we have a choice—resist and cling to what we know, or surrender and allow something extraordinary to unfold.

At the age of forty-five, deep in the jungles of Brazil, I faced my own moment of surrender—one that shattered the illusion of who I thought I was and set me on the path to remembering who I'd always been. That journey began inside this temazcal, an ancient sweat lodge used for purification and spiritual rebirth.

The Heat of Fear

We were crammed inside a low, domed enclosure—twenty of us, packed shoulder to shoulder in near-total darkness. Sweat slicked our bodies before the ceremony had even begun. In the center, a shallow pit held the glowing heart of the ritual—molten-hot stones, their surfaces pulsing red as the shaman carefully placed them one by one. These stones, known as *grandmothers*, were more than just sources of heat— they were honored as ancient keepers of wisdom, carriers of the Earth's memory, and sacred instruments of transformation.

As the shaman welcomed each one with reverence, murmuring words of gratitude, a wave of fear overtook me.

I was in a strange country, in a strange place, surrounded by people who didn't speak my language. The pungent scent of burning *palo santo* filled the air—thick, smoky, unfamiliar—intensifying my unease. To make matters worse, my wife sat on the opposite side of the temazcal, beyond my reach, beyond my sight. I couldn't see her. I had no way of knowing if she was okay, and that uncertainty gnawed at me.

The heat pressed in from all sides, and with every passing moment, my fear tightened its grip.

What made this ceremony even more dangerous was what had come before it. We had spent the entire day under the brutal sun, building the temazcal ourselves—clearing the forest floor, cutting down trees, bending and binding them into a low, domed frame, covering it in thick layers of blankets. The jungle heat was merciless, and by the time we finished, we were already severely dehydrated. Sweat had poured from my body in steady streams, and I had barely replaced what I lost. By the time we crawled inside the temazcal, my head was pounding, my mouth dry as dust.

The human body is remarkably resilient, but it has limits. A dry sauna at 150°F (65°C) is uncomfortable but manageable because sweat evaporates, cooling the skin. A temazcal, however, is different. The thick, humid air holds the heat, trapping it against your skin. Sweat no longer serves its purpose—it beads, pools, and clings to you, refusing to evaporate. Instead of cooling you down, it suffocates you under a layer of moisture.

At temperatures like these, dehydration becomes a real danger. I had already lost so much fluid building the temazcal under the relentless jungle sun. Now, inside this steaming womb of stone and sweat, my body was being pushed past its limits. My heart pounded, pumping blood furiously in a desperate attempt to regulate my core temperature. My head throbbed. My muscles ached.

I forced myself to take slow, deliberate breaths, but the air was thick, heavy—almost too dense to pull into my lungs. Every inhalation burned. Every exhalation seared.

Breaking Past the Threshold

I wasn't just uncomfortable. I was in danger.

At a core body temperature of 104°F (40°C), heatstroke sets in. The brain swells, confusion takes hold, and the organs begin to shut down. I didn't know my exact temperature, but I could feel myself approaching a threshold I had never crossed before. My body was no longer trying to cool itself—it was conserving what little strength it had left.

And yet, despite the physical suffering, I stayed.

I knew I could tap out at any moment. All I had to do was crawl to the door, push aside the heavy wool blanket, and collapse into the night air. But something deep inside me refused to move. A voice I couldn't yet name whispered, *Stay. Endure. Break through.*

I had spent my whole life avoiding discomfort, choosing control over uncertainty, and retreating the moment things became too painful, too unpredictable, too real. I had built an entire identity around strength, but the kind of strength that was about dominance, not endurance. I powered through challenges with sheer will, forcing outcomes, manipulating circumstances, and engineering success so that I never had to truly feel what it meant to struggle.

But this wasn't something I could outthink. There was no strategy, no shortcut, no way to muscle my way through. The temazcal was a mirror, reflecting back to me the truth I had been running from my entire life—I wasn't in control.

I thought about all the times I had run—when the discomfort became too much, when emotions felt like they might consume me, when situations demanded more vulnerability than I was willing to give. I had escaped into work, into achievement, into distractions that made me feel powerful but kept me disconnected. I had convinced myself that pushing forward was the same as facing things head-on. But now, sitting in this inferno, I realized they weren't the same at all.

The Test of Surrender

Indigenous elders taught that the way you enter and exit the temazcal reveals the way you move through life. Every stage of the ceremony became a mirror. Crawling inside wasn't just an entrance—it was an act of surrender, a willingness to strip away the illusion of control and step into the unknown. Inside, the heat and darkness became sacred forces of purification, peeling away the layers we all carry—the distractions, the defenses, the stories we cling to in order to feel safe. The temazcal doesn't just cleanse the body; it reveals the truth beneath our masks, our striving, our fear. And for me, that truth came fast and hard. There was no escape, no numbing, no negotiating—only the raw core of who I was when all the noise fell away. The temazcal, like life itself, demanded trust. Trust in the process. Trust in the discomfort. Trust that on the other side of the fire, something new awaited.

And in that moment, I saw the pattern laid bare. If I crawled out now, if I gave in to the fear and the pain, wasn't that exactly what I had done my whole life? Wasn't that the version of me I was trying to leave behind?

And I couldn't do that anymore.

I had spent my whole life running from discomfort. But here, inside this suffocating chamber of heat and darkness, there was nowhere left to run.

I was trapped. Not just inside the temazcal but inside myself. The walls of my mind closed in as tightly as the thick, humid air, and every instinct screamed for escape. But escape wasn't an option.

And now, with the heat pressing in and no way out, I understood: This wasn't just discomfort—it was a breaking point.

Forty-five minutes in, it had become unbearable. My skin was on fire. My breath came in sharp, shallow gulps. Desperate for relief, I reached down, scraping dirt from the forest floor and rubbing it onto my arms and chest, hoping the cool earth would pull some of the heat away. It barely helped.

The shaman's voice rose and fell in a hypnotic rhythm, his drum pounding like a heartbeat in the darkness. The songs he sang were raw, primal—chants that sounded like they had been passed down through generations, vibrating deep in my bones. The air was thick with sound, heat, and the weight of something ancient.

Then, commotion. A sudden shift in the tight space, hushed voices, movement. Someone had passed out. I strained to see, but the darkness swallowed everything. There was a hurried splash of water, a few murmured words, and then—silence. No frantic scramble, no rush to escape. Just a pause, a moment of stillness, and then the ceremony continued as if nothing had happened.

No one panicked. No one left.

It was as if this was normal.

I expected alarm, concern—something. But instead, the group remained steady, their breathing deep, their bodies still, as if passing out in a sweltering chamber was just part of the process. And maybe it was.

A chilling realization hit me—these people are crazy. Even if you pass out, you're staying in the temazcal.

I swallowed hard. I had come prepared to endure discomfort, but this was something else. The rules of the outside world didn't apply here. There were no safety nets, no easy exits. Here, surrender didn't mean escape—it meant having complete faith in the process, even if it pushed you past your limits.

Fifteen minutes later, the heavy wool blanket covering the small opening was lifted for the second time, and a rush of cool night air spilled into the temazcal. I inhaled desperately, straining to pull in as much of it as I could, my body clinging to the brief relief. For a fleeting moment, my fear subsided. Is it over? Is that the end of the ceremony?

But then, through the dim light, I saw them—five more molten-hot grandmothers, glowing red as they were carried into the center pit. My heart sank.

The opening closed, sealing us back into the suffocating darkness.

The heat surged once more, pressing down like a living force, and I realized with growing dread—it's not over. Not even close.

I wanted to scream. To claw my way out. To beg for just one gulp of fresh air. But no one else moved. No one else fought. Around me, they sat, surrendering to the inferno as if it were an embrace rather than an assault. And I wondered—*was I the only one who couldn't take it?*

I sank into the fear. It overtook my mind. It overtook my body. My chest tightened, my breath coming in short, panicked gasps.

The Vision

I was never a spiritual person. I had grown up Catholic, but for most of my life, I had questioned the existence of a higher power. I had sat through Sunday Mass as a kid, listened to the sermons, memorized the prayers, but none of it ever felt real to me. It was tradition, obligation—something I went through the motions of without ever feeling connected to it. As I got older, I drifted further from it, dismissing the idea of God as something for other people, something that had no real place in my life.

Yet in that moment, with the unbearable heat closing in and no escape in sight, I found myself praying—not out of faith but out of desperation.

Please, God. Please help me.

The words slipped from my mind before I could even register them, instinctive and raw. I wasn't reciting a memorized prayer. I wasn't thinking about doctrine or dogma. This wasn't calculated. It was primal —the cry of a man pushed to his breaking point.

I clenched my hands into fists, pressing them into the dirt beneath me, as if grounding myself to the earth would somehow tether me to something stronger than the panic rising in my chest. My heart pounded against my ribs, and I couldn't tell if it was from the heat or the fear. My body was failing me. My mind was unraveling. And all I could do was whisper a plea into the void, hoping—praying—that something, anything, would hear me.

I whispered that prayer at first, then repeated it over and over in my mind, like a mantra, like a lifeline. I didn't know who I was praying to—

God, the universe, the grandmothers themselves—but I needed something, anything, to pull me through.

Still, the heat raged on. The pressure didn't lift. Doubt crept in. *Is anyone listening? Is anything out there?*

My mind grasped for an exit, spinning through memories, through reasons, through anything that could make this moment feel less unbearable. But there was nowhere to go. No escape. Just the fire, the darkness, and the steady, rhythmic pounding of the shaman's drum. I thought of tapping out. Crawling to the door. Giving in.

But then, after the hundredth prayer, something happened.

The temazcal vanished.

The unbearable heat, the weight of the bodies pressed against me, the rhythmic drumbeats—all of it dissolved in an instant. One moment, I was trapped inside the suffocating darkness, my body teetering on the edge of collapse. The next, I was somewhere else entirely.

I looked around, disoriented. I was no longer inside the temazcal. The walls, the heat, the voices—they had all disappeared. Instead, I was sitting beneath an open sky—an endless stretch of black velvet dusted with stars, deeper and more infinite than any night I had ever seen. The stars weren't just distant pinpricks of light—they pulsed, alive, as if they were watching me, as if they had been waiting. The air was crisp and cool, filling my lungs like the first breath after nearly drowning. My body no longer ached. My mind was no longer unraveling.

For a moment, I wasn't searching. I wasn't panicking. I wasn't anything.

I just existed.

At first, I thought I had died. The transition had been so sudden, so absolute, that there was no other explanation. One second, I was suffocating inside the temazcal, my body on the verge of collapse. The next, I was sitting in an infinite, silent expanse.

I pressed my palms against the ground, feeling nothing and everything all at once. It wasn't solid, but it held me. It wasn't air, but I wasn't falling. I wasn't afraid. I wasn't anything.

And then, in the distance—movement. A shadow against the endless horizon, shifting, advancing.

A figure emerged, riding through the vast expanse with quiet authority. A Native American warrior astride a powerful horse, moving steadily toward me. As he approached, I saw the details sharpen—the strong, unyielding lines of his face, the large spear gripped firmly in his right hand. His horse stopped inches from me, its breath warm against my skin. Its nose, soft as brushed suede, twitched slightly as it exhaled, the scent of earth and sweat filling the space between us. The fine hairs along its muzzle caught the faint light, shifting with each breath.

I looked up, locking eyes with the man above me, and something inside me shifted. It wasn't just that he was strong—he *was* strength. An unshakable force. Power. Presence. A fearlessness so absolute, it didn't need to be announced or proven. It simply *was*. He radiated it in a way that made words unnecessary, his very existence a testament to something beyond courage—something closer to inevitability, as if he had never known another way to be.

His gaze was steady, unyielding. There was no judgment in his eyes, no challenge—only knowing. As if he had seen men like me before. As if he already understood why I was here, what I had been running from, and what I needed to learn.

Time stretched between us, silent and weighty, until finally, his voice broke through the stillness. Deep. Grounded. Steady as stone.

"Fear is worse than death, and that is why I fear no death."

The words didn't just land. They *cut*. They carved through me, through every excuse, every hesitation, every silent fear I had carried for so long. They reverberated through my body, through my very soul.

In that suspended moment, I saw with complete clarity how fear had held me back—fear of the unknown, fear of failure, fear of discomfort, fear of stepping fully into my purpose. It wasn't just a feeling—it had been the architect of my entire life, dictating my choices, shaping my identity, keeping me small when something greater had always been calling. The warrior stood before me as living proof that courage was not the absence of fear but the mastery of it. He was not untouched by fear—he had simply refused to let it rule him.

Then, without hesitation, he and his horse began to move.

Not around me. *Through* me.

I didn't flinch. I didn't move. I couldn't. My body was frozen, yet I felt everything—his energy merging with mine, his strength flooding into me as if I were a hollow vessel being filled for the first time. His spear passed through my chest, yet there was no pain. His horse's hooves struck the ground where my feet should have been, yet I remained still. The air around me vibrated, my skin prickling as if lightning had just passed through my bones.

And then, in an instant, he was inside me.

A jolt shot through my spine—a heat unlike anything I had felt before. Not the external burn of the temazcal, but something internal, something ancient, something alive. It coursed through me, rewiring, reconfiguring, dissolving the walls I had built around myself for years.

Every part of me that had clung to fear—every doubt, every hesitation, every excuse—shattered like brittle glass. My body pulsed with a force I had never known, my chest expanding as if it could no longer contain all that I was becoming. I could feel the warrior's presence inside me, not as something separate but as something I had always been. His certainty. His power. His absolute refusal to be controlled by anything other than his own will.

I was no longer just *me*.

I was him.

I was everything I had been too afraid to become.

And then, there was nothing.

Emerging Reborn

I sat in that sacred stillness for another hour, unmoving, untouched by time or space, completely at peace. The heat still pressed against my skin, but it no longer burned. The air was still thick, but I no longer fought to breathe. The darkness was absolute, but I was not lost in it. For the first time in my life, I wasn't seeking an escape. I wasn't searching for a way out, for relief, for something outside of myself to make it better.

I simply *was*.

The warrior's presence lingered within me, not as a memory but as an undeniable part of who I now was. The energy he carried—his fearlessness, his stillness, his absolute certainty—had settled into my bones, like a forgotten truth finally remembered.

I felt no urgency to move. No need to shift. I sat cross-legged on the dirt floor, my hands resting lightly on my knees, my breath slow and steady. There was no mind chatter. No doubt. No thought at all. Just an overwhelming presence, a feeling of complete belonging within myself.

The temazcal had transformed from a suffocating furnace into something else entirely—a womb, holding me in its darkness, allowing me to dissolve and be remade. I had entered this space desperate, gasping, clinging to an identity that was breaking apart under the weight of my own illusions. But now, there was nothing left to hold on to. And I wasn't afraid.

I don't know how much time passed. It could have been minutes, hours, eternity. Nothing existed beyond this moment, this breath, this being.

Then, somewhere beyond the walls, I faintly heard movement—shuffling feet, voices carried by the night air. The ceremony had ended. People were leaving, stepping back into the world outside.

And yet, I remained.

I could have stayed there forever.

Eventually, someone must have realized I was missing. Maybe they assumed I had run off into the jungle like a madman—because who in their right mind would willingly stay inside the temazcal once the door had been opened? Or maybe they had felt something—an absence where I should have been. A presence that had gone too deep.

Someone had the foresight to crawl back inside.

I felt a hand on my arm—warm, insistent. A grip, firm but not forceful. A tug, pulling me back from wherever I had gone.

And in an instant, my trance was shattered.

The stillness fractured like glass, and suddenly, I was back. The heat rushed in again, thick and stifling. The damp earth beneath me was real again, pressing into my skin. My body felt heavy, weighted, as if I had just returned from a place beyond the edges of the world.

I blinked, my eyes adjusting to the absolute darkness, but I still couldn't see.

Another tug on my arm.

I allowed myself to be pulled, crawling forward blindly until the thick wool blanket was lifted. I emerged, slow and deliberate, stepping out onto the damp earth. The night sky stretched above me, impossibly vast, and for a moment, I simply stood there, breathing it in.

The cool air wrapped around me, covering my skin, soothing the raw heat that still clung to my body. My chest rose and fell in slow, deliberate breaths, as if I were learning how to inhale again, how to exist in this world outside the temazcal. Everything felt sharper—the scent of damp earth, the distant chirping of insects, the glow of the moon casting silver light across the jungle. I could feel every pulse of life around me, every shift in the air. It was as if my senses had been stripped down and rewired, recalibrated to something deeper, something truer.

I took a slow step forward, then another, my feet sinking slightly into the soft ground. My body was still radiating heat, as if the fire inside the temazcal had fused with my very being. My muscles ached, my skin glistened with sweat, but I felt *light*, weightless in a way I had never known before.

And then, I saw her.

Brooks, my wife, was sitting on a log near the stream, her posture relaxed, yet there was an intensity in her stillness. The firelight flickered against her skin, illuminating the soft edges of her face, the curve of her shoulder. She was staring out at the water, her expression unreadable, yet I knew—without words, without explanation—that she had been through her own transformation inside that temazcal.

She must have sensed me, because she turned, her eyes finding mine in the dim glow of the moonlight. For a moment, we simply looked at each other.

No words. No need for them.

I walked to her slowly, my legs still adjusting to solid ground, and without hesitation, she opened her arms. I collapsed into them, sinking against her, feeling the warmth of her body against mine. She wrapped her arms around me, and I held her just as tightly.

We sat like that for what felt like forever.

The world around us disappeared. There was no past, no future, no need to explain what had just happened inside that temazcal. There was only *this*—this moment, this breath, this undeniable connection between us. Our bodies still pulsed with heat, but neither of us moved to cool ourselves. We just let it be.

For the next thirty minutes, we sat in silence, arms wrapped around each other, grounding ourselves in the moment. The sounds of the jungle hummed around us—the rustling leaves, the gentle trickle of the stream, the distant murmur of voices from the others. But none of it intruded.

I had never experienced a moment so raw, so tender, so profoundly *shared*.

To go through something like that with the most important person in my life—it was priceless.

It was as if we had both been stripped down to our essence, our masks burned away, our walls dissolved. And here we were, just *us*, in the purest form possible.

Nothing between us.

Nothing left to prove.

Only love. Only presence. Only this.

The Shaman's Message

After the temazcal, we all gathered inside the main building and sat in a circle. A single candle flickered at the center of the room, casting long shadows across the walls, as if the spirits of the ceremony still lingered among us.

The shaman took his place at the top of the group, his presence commanding yet serene. He swept his gaze over us, his eyes carrying the weight of generations of wisdom. With a simple nod, he invited each of us to share our experience.

One by one, people spoke. Some described the unbearable heat, the feeling of suffocation, the moment they thought they wouldn't make it. Others spoke of visions—ancestors appearing before them, messages whispered through the steam, sensations of floating between realms. A few wept openly, the intensity of the experience still unraveling inside them.

The shaman listened intently. After each person spoke, he responded—not with generic affirmations but with insights so precise, so deeply attuned to the speaker's truth, that it was as if he had peered directly into their soul. He didn't just hear their words—he saw them:

the unspoken fears, the buried pain, the transformation still unfolding within them. He spoke with a certainty that felt ancient, as if he were reading something written deep inside them, something they had not yet learned to read themselves. He told them things that only they would understand, piercing through their confusion and doubt with a clarity that was almost unsettling. It was as if he knew them better than they knew themselves, unpacking their experiences in ways they hadn't yet been able to articulate.

I sat there, listening, absorbing, watching how each person unraveled in their own way. Some had revelations that seemed to crack them open. Others left with more questions than answers. But every single one of them had been *seen*—and that, in itself, was its own kind of healing.

As the circle moved closer to me, I felt the weight of what had just happened inside the temazcal pressing against my chest. My heart pounded, not from nerves but from the sheer impossibility of trying to explain what I had just experienced.

How could I possibly put it into words?

I had entered that sweat lodge as one version of myself and emerged as something . . . else. Transformed. *Stripped down.* I had seen a warrior. I had felt him *become* me. I had walked out of that temazcal different, yet I still didn't fully understand *how*.

I clenched my hands into fists, feeling the dried dirt still caked under my nails. My throat tightened. The words simply *weren't there*.

And then, suddenly, it was my turn.

I opened my mouth to speak, ready to deliver my thoughts in the way I always had—concise, clear, to the point. I was no stranger to public speaking. Words had always come easily to me, shaped with precision and intention. I had spent a lifetime perfecting the ability to say exactly what I meant, exactly how I wanted to say it—to present myself in a certain way. Controlled. Composed. In command of the narrative.

But as soon as I tried, something inside me cracked wide open.

My voice broke. My chest tightened. Tears surged before I could stop them. I had no control over it. No way to compose myself, no way to neatly package the experience into something logical or presentable. The tears came in uncontrollable waves, my body heaving with sobs I couldn't suppress. And the more I tried to pull myself together, the more it overtook me.

After twenty years of marriage, Brooks had never seen me cry. Not once. Crying had never been part of my emotional vocabulary.

Yet here I was, surrounded by strangers, completely unraveled. I could feel Brooks beside me, feel the weight of her presence, but I couldn't look at her. I couldn't look at anyone. I wasn't just crying—I was *breaking open.*

The warrior. The fear. The surrender. The stillness. It was all still there, just beneath the surface, and the moment I reached for it, the dam collapsed. Sobs wracked my body, raw and unfiltered, each breath a struggle between release and restraint. My shoulders shook. My throat clenched. My breath came in ragged gasps.

I felt exposed in a way I never had before. Vulnerable. Raw. But at the same time, I wasn't ashamed. I wasn't scrambling to shove it all back down. It was as if something had been stripped away in that temazcal— something I had spent my entire life holding on to—and all that was left was the truth.

I wasn't sure how long I sat there, trembling, my chest rising and falling in uneven waves. The room around me blurred. It was like I was still somewhere between worlds—one foot in the temazcal, one foot here. My mind struggled to catch up with what my body already knew —something had shifted. Something irreversible.

I wiped my face with the back of my hand, trying to steady myself. I had spoken thousands of times in my life—boardrooms, conferences, even to rooms filled with hundreds of people. But this was different. There was no preparing for this. No crafting the perfect response. Just the raw, unfiltered truth sitting heavy in my chest, demanding to be spoken.

I finally choked out the last words of my story, my breath still uneven, my body drained. And then I sat back, exhausted, waiting for the shaman's response. I had just bared my soul. Surely, he would have something profound to say—some interpretation, some insight, something to help me process this earth-shattering moment.

But instead, he simply nodded.

Then he turned to the next person.

WTF?!

I sat there stunned. Dazed. Confused. *That's it?* I had just experienced something beyond my comprehension, something that left me sobbing like a child, and all I got was a nod? No explanation? No guidance? No reassurance that what had just happened to me *meant something*?

My mind scrambled to make sense of it, to assign some kind of meaning to the silence. Had I said too much? Not enough? Did he even understand the words between my sobs? Had I misread the entire experience? My chest was still heaving, my body still vibrating with the aftershocks of whatever had just broken open inside me, and yet . . . nothing. It was as if I had poured my heart out into a void.

My confusion twisted into something else—pure embarrassment. I had just broken down in front of my wife and a room full of strangers, exposing a part of myself I had spent a lifetime keeping hidden. And in response? A simple nod. No acknowledgment, no insight, nothing. I sat there, stunned, the rawness of my emotions still coursing through me, unsure of what I had expected—but it wasn't this.

To make matters worse, the woman next to me casually mentioned how hot she had been, and suddenly, the shaman leaned in, offering a long, thoughtful reflection on her journey. I sat there blinking, my mind struggling to process the absurdity of it. So sweating too much warranted deep introspection, but my complete emotional collapse was met with nothing?

I felt heat rise to my face, an uncomfortable mix of self-consciousness and regret. Had I said the wrong thing? Had I looked weak? I wanted to disappear, to shrink back into the version of myself who knew how to control the narrative.

But before I could fully process my frustration, the circle finished and the shaman stood up and walked straight toward me. He placed his hands firmly on my shoulders and stared into my eyes.

"You were born in February," he said.

I blinked, caught off guard. "Yes . . ." I said hesitantly. My mind scrambled for an explanation. He didn't know anything about me. I had never met this man before. How the hell did he know when I was born?

His gaze didn't waver. "What day?" he asked. I told him.

He nodded again. "I too was born on that day in February," he said. "We were born outside of the matrix. We can see through the illusions and experience life on a spiritual level."

I stood frozen, unable to respond. A part of me instinctively understood what he was saying, but another part of me was light-years away from that truth. It was like we weren't just talking—we were communicating on some deeper, unspoken level.

Something about the way he looked at me—unblinking, unwavering—made it impossible to dismiss his words. He wasn't speaking in riddles. He wasn't trying to impress me with spiritual clichés. He was stating a fact, as if he had peered into the very core of my being and seen something I hadn't yet recognized in myself.

Then he said the words that shattered me. "You must release control and learn to surrender."

And just like that, I lost it.

Tears poured from my eyes, unbidden and unstoppable. His words didn't just touch something inside me—they detonated it. It was as if they bypassed my intellect entirely, striking straight at the deepest part of me, the part I had spent a lifetime fortifying against weakness, uncertainty, and the unknown.

In that moment, I became hyper-aware of the tightness in my body —the constant tension I had carried for as long as I could remember. My jaw, always clenched. My shoulders, perpetually tight. My stomach, unconsciously contracted even when I was at rest. I could feel the weight of the control I had been gripping with white-knuckled intensity, the way I had micromanaged, strategized, and *forced* my way through life.

Control wasn't just how I operated—it was who I was. It was how I had survived, how I had built, how I had *won*. I had ruled my world with an unshakable belief that I was the architect of my own destiny, that my fate was mine and mine alone to dictate. I had always trusted my ability to outwork, outthink, and outmaneuver any obstacle in my path.

But now? Standing there, undone in front of this man?

It hit me like a tidal wave—*I was exhausted.*

Exhausted from the endless effort. Exhausted from holding everything together. Exhausted from the illusion that if I just controlled more, did more, pushed harder, I would finally feel whole. But no matter how much I achieved, no matter how much I built, there was always more to control. More to protect. More to manage.

And now, here was this man—this shaman, this stranger—telling me to let go.

I didn't even know what surrender really meant.

Surrender had always felt like defeat to me. Like losing. Like weakness. And weakness? That wasn't an option. Weakness meant failure. Weakness meant being at the mercy of forces I couldn't control. Weakness meant vulnerability.

But as I stood there, stripped raw, tears streaming down my face, something deep inside me whispered:

What if surrender isn't weakness? What if it's freedom?

I didn't have an answer.

But I knew, with every fiber of my being, that this wasn't the last time I would hear those words.

Surrender—true surrender—would become the most important lesson of my life.

The Awakening

After my experience in Brazil, I woke up—not in the physical sense, but in a way that shook me to my core. It was as if a veil had been lifted, revealing the truth that I had been hijacked by an invisible algorithm running in the background of my life, dictating my every decision without my awareness. I had become trapped in an identity that wasn't truly mine, blind to how my choices were rooted in fear—fear of not succeeding, fear of my children not reaching their full potential, fear of disappointing those around me. Fear of being vulnerable. Fear of not presenting a perfect image. Fear of being undesirable. Fear of being unloved.

This realization hit me like a slap across the face. It was undeniable, and I became obsessed with understanding how I had ended up here. How had I allowed fear and the constant threat of failure to dictate my every move? For years, I had believed I was in control, but the truth was, I had been operating from a place of deep, unconscious insecurity.

I could feel—deep in my bones—that there was something bigger than me. Something pushing and pulling me out of my carefully constructed comfort zone and into the unknown. Into discomfort. Into growth.

So many questions. So few answers. But it was that hunger for understanding that led me down a path of self-discovery—one that would force me to confront old wounds, challenge long-held beliefs, and embark on a journey of transformation and awareness that would bring me to the most uncomfortable of places. And it would be there, in my most uncomfortable places, that I would find my greatest life lessons.

But the first question that burned in my mind was this: How did I get here?

Building the temazcal—bending branches, layering blankets, and preparing for the intense ceremony ahead.

The completed temazcal—a gray dome in the jungle, where heat, darkness, and ritual pushed me to my edge and beyond.

2

THE ILLUSION OF ENOUGH

"When we are no longer able to change a situation, we are challenged to change ourselves."
—Viktor Frankl

I grew up in Indianapolis in the early 1980s—the youngest of four kids, in a time when kids roamed the neighborhood freely until families sat down for dinner without the distraction of cell phones or social media. By all accounts, my childhood was idyllic—a safe, steady world shaped by two loving parents who believed that hard work and integrity were not just values but the foundation of a meaningful life.

My Father—Discipline as a Way of Life

My father was a banker, a man who had built his career from nothing, rising through sheer determination and an unshakable moral code. He had come from very modest means, and rather than seeing his background as a limitation, he treated it as fuel. He was the kind of man who didn't just believe in hard work—he embodied it. He operated by a simple, unwavering principle: *You say what you mean, and you do what you say.* There was no need for grand declarations or self-congratulation —his actions spoke for him. He didn't believe in excuses, in half-measures, or in bending the truth to make things easier. His word was a contract, not just with others but with himself.

As a banker, he had an impeccable judgment of character. Numbers and financial statements mattered, of course, but he understood that a person's true creditworthiness wasn't just on paper—it was in their integrity, their work ethic, their ability to follow through on their commitments. If he believed in you, if he saw something in you that couldn't be captured by a balance sheet, he would take a chance. He would approve a loan even when the data might suggest otherwise.

His customers knew this. And through his work at the bank, he changed people's lives. There were people who walked into his office with nothing but an idea and the drive to make it real, and because he saw their potential—because he believed in them when others wouldn't —they walked out with the capital to build something lasting.

I didn't fully grasp the impact of this until years later. We went to the Indianapolis 500 every year, one of the biggest traditions in our city. While thousands of people sat in miles-long lines, waiting for hours to get in, my father always had us join a police escort straight through the traffic, bypassing the chaos like we were dignitaries. It wasn't until much later that I learned the truth behind that privilege.

A man who had once come to my father for a loan—someone the bank's numbers probably wouldn't have approved—had built his small business into a massive company. That loan had been the catalyst. It had given him the chance to build something that mattered. And he never forgot who had believed in him when it counted. He was the one who invited my father to join that VIP escort every year as a quiet, unspoken thank-you.

But my father never mentioned it. He never took credit, never sought praise for his good deeds or accomplishments. He sat on boards of nonprofits, helping to shape Indianapolis into the thriving city it was becoming, yet he never boasted about the role he played.

He wasn't in it for recognition. He never chased prestige. He simply did what he believed was right. And that, more than anything, was the example I grew up with.

Honesty wasn't just a virtue to him—it was nonnegotiable. He held himself to a standard so high, it sometimes felt impossible to reach, and he expected the same from everyone around him. If he told you he was going to do something, it was as good as done. If he set a goal, he would achieve it. No complaints, no excuses, no second-guessing.

But what struck me most about my father wasn't just his work ethic —it was his discipline. He wasn't the type to get swept up in whims or emotions. If he wanted to change a habit, he simply decided—and then he followed through, with the same steady resolve that he applied to everything else in life. I watched him wake up at the same time every morning and carry himself through each day with relentless consistency. It was as if his mind and body had been trained to obey his will, without resistance, without hesitation.

I was in awe of his ability to commit to something and see it through, no matter how difficult. It was a quality I deeply admired but struggled to embody myself.

The Pull of Instant Gratification

If my father was the embodiment of discipline, I was its opposite. My young mind craved dopamine—the rush of instant gratification. Where he found comfort in structure and routine, I found it stifling. I wanted excitement, adventure, and shortcuts to success.

I was the kid who was drawn to the thrill of the moment—sneaking in extra time playing video games, avoiding homework until the last possible second (or not doing it at all), and constantly pushing boundaries at school simply because I was bored. If there was a way to get the reward without the work, I wanted to find it. If there was a way to win without struggling, I was determined to figure it out.

And yet, despite my constant search for shortcuts, I couldn't escape the shadow of my father's example. His iron will, his unshakable integrity, his ability to push through discomfort without complaint—it was impossible to ignore. Even as I rebelled against it in my youth, a part of me knew—one day, I'll have to figure this out. One day, I'll have to become more like him.

I just didn't know how.

But I wanted to. More than anything, I wanted to make him proud. That was something I longed for my entire life.

So I did what I thought he would do. When we arrived home from a trip, I jumped out of the car first, grabbing the bags so the women wouldn't have to. At the gas station, I pumped the gas for my mother, just as I had seen him do. I opened doors for women, always mindful of the example he had set.

None of it came naturally to me. I wasn't disciplined like he was. I wasn't wired for patience or self-restraint. But I forced myself to try because I wanted, more than anything, to live up to him.

The Quiet Force of a Mother's Love

My mother was a gem. Smart, exceptionally beautiful, dedicated to her family, and possessing an aura that intimidated those who didn't know her well. There was a quiet power in the way she carried herself—a presence that commanded attention without ever needing to demand it. She was the kind of woman who could walk into a room and shift the energy with nothing more than a glance. People listened when she spoke, not just because of what she said but because of how she said it— with conviction, intelligence, and an unwavering sense of certainty.

She woke up early every morning, long before the rest of us, moving through the house with a quiet efficiency. By the time my father and siblings came downstairs, breakfast was already prepared, our bags were packed, and everything we needed for the day was in place. It wasn't just about keeping the house running—it was an act of devotion, a way of ensuring that we started our days knowing we were cared for.

Every morning, without fail, she drove us to school. And every afternoon, she was there to pick us up. It didn't matter how busy she was, what obligations she had, or how many other things demanded her attention—she showed up. Every day. She made it look effortless, but looking back, I see it for what it truly was—an unwavering commitment to being present, to making sure we knew that no matter what happened in the outside world, we could always count on her.

But my mother was never just a homemaker. She was a force. She served on high school and university boards, dedicating her time to making the world around her better. She had opinions, strong ones, and she never hesitated to voice them. She could go toe-to-toe with anyone —administrators, other board members—and she did, often. She believed in fairness, in standing up for what was right, not just for herself or for us but for everyone. And yet, despite all of that, she never boasted. She never needed validation or applause. She simply did what needed to be done.

I remember when I was younger attending a big, formal event where my mother was being honored for her work on a board. I remember sitting there, watching as people stood at a podium and spoke about her contributions, and thinking, Who is this woman? And what exactly did she do?

She was so focused on us, always asking about our lives, making sure we were okay, that she never talked about herself or her accomplishments. It struck me, in that moment, how little I actually knew about the work she had been doing. I felt bad—guilty even—that I had never really asked my mom what she did. It wasn't that I didn't care, but she made it easy not to ask. She never sought attention, never brought it up. She was content to do the work, to make an impact quietly, without the need for recognition.

As a mother, she was always there. Always loving. But firm. She was not the type to coddle, nor did she indulge excuses. When she said something, she meant it. And when she set an expectation, you met it. There were no empty threats, no idle warnings. If she said you'd lose privileges for misbehaving, you lost them. If she told you to be home at a certain time, you were home at that time—no exceptions, no debates. She wasn't harsh, but she was unwavering. Her discipline wasn't about control—it was about teaching responsibility, self-respect, and an understanding that actions had consequences.

She often reminded me, "I'm your mother, not your best friend," a distinction she upheld with both grace and conviction. There was no blurring of lines, no playing favorites. She loved fiercely, but it was a love that held you accountable, that wouldn't let you off the hook. She was not strict for the sake of being strict but because she saw your potential and refused to let you settle for anything less.

I never wanted to disappoint her.

Her approval, like my father's, wasn't something I just wanted—it was something I needed. It became the measuring stick for my worth, the standard against which I judged myself. If she was proud of me, I had done something right. If she was disappointed, I had failed—not just in her eyes but in my own. And yet, the pressure wasn't overt. She never burdened me with expectations, never demanded perfection, never compared me to others. She simply carried herself in a way that made me want to rise to her level.

I wasn't driven by pressure—I was driven by the quiet, undeniable power of my parents' example. They didn't demand excellence. They embodied it. They lived with discipline, integrity, and an unwavering commitment to their values. And in my young mind, anything less than that wasn't just failure—it was unworthiness. It wasn't about winning trophies or earning accolades—it was about proving, through my actions, that I was worthy of their love. That I was worthy of being their son.

The Legacy of Greatness

Unlike my father, my mother came from wealth. Her father—my grandfather—was an incredible businessman who took their family business and turned it into a global enterprise. But he was more than just successful—he was a visionary, a man who saw opportunities where others saw obstacles. He built something that would last beyond his lifetime, something that would provide not just for his family but for entire communities. His story became legendary in our family—a tale of discipline, tireless effort, and relentless pursuit of excellence.

A hardworking Catholic family, they had grown up in a small Indiana town, where discipline, hard work, giving back to the community, and living with absolute honesty and integrity weren't just ideals—they were the only way to live. My grandfather's word was his bond, and he built his business not just on intelligence and strategy but on trust. People believed in him because he was unwavering in his values. As a child, I would hear stories of my grandfather walking away from lucrative business deals because a politician wanted a kickback or an administrator expected a bribe. He wouldn't argue. He wouldn't try to negotiate. He would simply stand up, shake their hand, and walk away, no matter how much money was on the table. To him, there was no gray area—if someone's integrity could be bought, they weren't worth doing business with.

His reputation preceded him. People knew that if they wanted to work with my grandfather, they had to do it the right way. There were no shortcuts, no under-the-table deals, no bending the rules to make things easier. And while other businessmen might have justified a compromise here or there for the sake of growth, he never did. He believed that success wasn't what you built—it was *how* you built it.

Honesty and integrity were hammered into us from generation to generation. In our family, there was no such thing as cutting corners. No such thing as easy success. If you wanted to build something great, you had to earn it.

And he had the same standards and expectations for his employees. His salespeople would meet with him once per year to receive their salary for the entire year—all at once. No biweekly paychecks, no direct deposits. Just one lump sum.

He believed, *"If they can't manage their own finances, how can they manage mine?"*

It was a test but also a statement of trust. He expected his employees to be as disciplined with their own money as they were with his business. To him, financial responsibility wasn't just a personal matter—it was a reflection of a person's integrity, their ability to plan, to think long-term, to resist the temptation of quick rewards in favor of sustained success. He was doing more than simply building a company—he was shaping people who could be trusted, people who carried themselves with the same level of accountability that he did.

And if they couldn't? Well, they wouldn't be working for him much longer.

Chasing a Giant

My grandfather was a role model for me and all the grandchildren. The men in the family wanted to be like him. I myself have spent my entire life chasing him, striving to be as successful and meaningful to the world as he was. I watched the way my uncles, my cousins, and even my mother spoke about him—with deep admiration, almost reverence. He wasn't the kind of man who filled silence just to be heard. When he spoke, his words carried weight. They meant something. People listened —not out of obligation but because they knew his wisdom was earned, his advice worth taking.

I wanted that.

I wanted to be the person whose words mattered, the person others turned to for guidance. The kind of man whose presence alone commanded respect, not because he demanded it but because he had built a life worthy of it.

Through his accomplishments, he instilled in me this notion of unlimited potential. His life was proof that success wasn't just for the lucky or the privileged—it was for those who were willing to work for it. And through my need to be perfect and fill my grandfather's shoes, I turned his success into my ultimate benchmark. I wanted to follow in his footsteps, yes—but more than that, I wanted to prove I was worthy of them.

But there was a difference. He never had to prove his worth—he simply was who he was. He lived by his principles, and success followed. For me, success felt like something I had to chase, something I had to earn, something that could be taken away if I didn't measure up. His accomplishments were more than inspiring—they became the standard against which I measured my own value. If I couldn't achieve what he had, if I fell short in any way, then who was I?

The weight of that expectation, though never explicitly placed on me, became the foundation of my identity. No one in my family ever sat me down and told me that I had to be just like my grandfather. No one said I had to reach the same heights, build the same kind of empire, or leave the same kind of mark on the world. But I felt it anyway. It was in the stories we told about him, the way people spoke his name, the way his presence loomed over our family gatherings even after he was gone.

I found myself not only striving for success but fighting to justify my place—to prove that I was enough. That belief shaped everything, even the dreams I held as a child. It was never about wealth. It was about meaning. About impact. About making sure that when my name was spoken in the future, it carried the same weight, the same respect, the same legacy.

And so, from the time I was young, I set my sights on something bigger than myself. I didn't just want to build a business—I wanted to build an empire. I didn't just want to be good at something—I wanted to be great. Anything less than that wasn't an option. Because in my mind, success wasn't just a goal. It was proof. Proof that I was worth something. Proof that I was worth loving.

The Mirage of Success

Looking back, I can see that ambition for what it was—a mirage. The illusion that success would finally bring me the love, security, and sense of belonging I craved. That if I could just win enough, prove enough, build something big enough, then maybe I would feel whole.

It wasn't a conscious belief. It was more like a hidden operating system running in the background, dictating my every move. And like a mirage in the desert, no matter how much I chased it, it always moved further away.

For years, I told myself the next achievement would be the one. The one that finally made me feel like I had arrived. The one that silenced the relentless voice whispering, *Not enough. Keep going. Do more. Be more.* I believed if I could just reach the next milestone—whether it was a bigger deal, a more successful company, or an accolade that proved my worth—then maybe I would feel the peace that had always eluded me.

But that moment never came.

No matter how much I achieved, I never felt truly satisfied. Almost —but never quite. Success had an ever-moving finish line, receding just as I approached it. I didn't know why.

I had seen people who carried themselves with a kind of ease I couldn't understand. People who weren't playing the same high-stakes game yet seemed deeply content. They weren't chasing something—they just *were*. And that confused me.

Because my whole life had been built on the belief that success was the key to happiness. That once I got *there*—wherever *there* was—then I could finally relax, finally enjoy life, finally feel worthy.

But I never stopped to ask the real question: *What if success isn't the answer? What if the thing I'm chasing isn't the thing that will save me?*

At the time, I wasn't ready to ask that question.

So I did what I had always done. I ran faster. I set bigger goals. I convinced myself that the next milestone would be the one to change everything. I didn't realize yet that I was trapped in a cycle—one that would never end until I had the courage to stop running and finally turn inward.

The Fear Equation

I thought I was driven by ambition. But the truth is, I was driven by fear.

Fear of not being enough. Fear of falling short. Fear that if I stopped striving for even a second, I'd prove to the world—and to myself—that I wasn't worthy of the love and validation I so deeply craved.

I had spent my life convinced that my relentless pursuit of achievement was fueled by passion, by an unstoppable will to win. But in reality, I wasn't chasing greatness—I was running from the shame of not being *great enough*.

Every success was like a quick fix—a fleeting moment of relief before the emptiness crept back in, whispering, *It still isn't enough.*

So I pushed harder. The next deal. The next milestone. The next win.

Each time, I told myself, *This will be the one.* The one that makes me feel whole. The one that silences the doubt, the fear, the gnawing sense that I was always just one misstep away from proving myself a fraud.

But no matter how many times I crossed the finish line, the feeling of attainment never lasted.

Because the truth was, I had built a game I could never win.

No matter how fast I ran, no matter how much I achieved, the goalpost kept moving.

And I didn't yet realize that the thing I was chasing had never been out there.

It had been inside me all along.

3

THE PRISON OF BECOMING

"You are the prisoner, the prison, and the prison keeper. Only you hold the key."

—Adrienne Posey

Brazil changed everything. For the first time in my life, I became aware—*truly* aware. Aware that I had been living in a prison of my own making. Aware that my mind had been hijacked by an unconscious program, running me on autopilot, keeping me trapped in an endless loop of fear and striving. Aware that my suffering wasn't coming from the outside world but was entirely self-inflicted—born from my fixation on a future that didn't exist.

I had spent my life lost in a relentless pursuit of *what's next*, believing that happiness, fulfillment, and peace were just over the next hill—after the next deal, the next achievement, the next success. But the future is an illusion, an ever-moving finish line that recedes the closer you get. No matter how much you achieve, it never feels like enough, because the mind—conditioned to chase—never allows itself to arrive.

The Paradox of Seeking

When I wasn't trapped in the future, I was chained to the past. Every regret, every mistake, every moment when I had fallen short played on repeat, reinforcing the belief that I wasn't enough. My mind would resurrect old failures as proof, keeping me locked in an invisible battle between who I *had been* and who I *needed to become*. And the harder I fought to close that gap, the wider it seemed to grow.

The more desperately I sought to become successful, the more elusive success felt. The more I chased fulfillment, the further it drifted from reach. It was as if my wanting—my constant striving—was the very force pushing it all away. Like trying to catch my own shadow, the act of pursuit itself ensured I would never grasp what I was looking for.

The moment we declare that we want something, we reinforce the belief that we lack it. If I tell myself I need to become worthy, I affirm that I am not worthy now. If I chase happiness, I confirm that happiness is not here. The mind, in its endless need to achieve, unknowingly creates the very suffering it hopes to escape.

This is the paradox of seeking—the more we chase something, the more we affirm its absence. Desire, by its very nature, is rooted in lack. It tricks us into believing that fulfillment lies just beyond our reach, in some future moment, some external achievement, some next milestone. And so we run—toward success, toward love, toward peace—always hoping that the next thing will finally complete us. But the more we seek, the further away the answer seems to move.

This is why people who seek happiness often find themselves anxious and discontent. Why those who chase love often feel unworthy of it. Why those who strive for success never feel like they've arrived. The very act of seeking keeps us locked in a cycle of never having.

The paradox is this—what we are seeking is often already here, but our belief in its absence keeps us from seeing it. We look outward, thinking the answer exists somewhere external to us, when in reality, it is our very search that blinds us to the truth.

Trapped in the Loop

I had spent my entire life seeking something—success, worthiness, meaning—never realizing that in my pursuit, I was reinforcing the belief that I didn't already have those things within me. And so, I remained trapped in the illusion of lack.

My life became a loop—chasing, striving, pushing—never realizing that the peace, the worth, the success I was so desperate to attain could never be found in the future. Because the future is an illusion. The more I reached for it, the more it slipped through my fingers. And the more I tried to *become*, the more I confirmed that I was *not enough* as I was.

This realization hit me like a freight train, and I became obsessed with the one thing I had spent my entire life avoiding—the present moment.

Confronting the Voices

I had always focused on the next step, the next achievement, the next version of myself, never once stopping to truly exist in *now*. But if the future was an illusion and the past was unchangeable, then what else was there?

This question consumed me, pulling me toward meditation, a practice I had once dismissed as pointless stillness. But now I wasn't looking for an edge, an outcome, or a strategy—I was looking for *truth*. I wanted to understand what existed beyond the relentless noise of my mind, beyond the endless loop of becoming. And so, I sat in silence. At first, it was unbearable. The silence wasn't empty—it was filled with voices, the same voices that had been running my life from the shadows. But now, without the constant distraction of work, goals, and endless striving, I could actually *hear* them. I was aware, and it felt like I was trapped in a room with a family of lunatics, each one shouting over the other, reminding me of every failure, every shortcoming, every reason I would never be enough.

You're not working hard enough.
You'll never be as successful as your grandfather.
If you slow down, you'll fall behind.

Who do you think you are?
What are you, some sort of a guru now? You're a total fake.

These voices weren't new. They had always been there, whispering just below the surface, fueling my relentless need to prove myself. But now, stripped of my usual escapes, they were deafening. I wanted to run, to drown them out with work, distractions, anything—but there was nowhere left to hide.

The Impossible Chase

The more I meditated, the more these voices consumed my thoughts. I did feel like a poser. I wanted so badly to be "the monk on the mountain", effortlessly clearing my thoughts, finding perfect stillness. But that very desire—the need to be something—only widened the gap between who I was and who I thought I should be.

The paradox of seeking is that the answers we desperately chase often exist right in front of us, waiting for us to recognize them. But when self-doubt clouds our vision, even the brightest truth can go unnoticed. I spent years searching for validation, for proof that I was enough. Yet, there was someone who had already found that proof— someone who believed in me long before I could believe in myself. At the time, I didn't understand what that meant. I didn't yet see that love itself can be a kind of mirror, reflecting back the parts of us we refuse to acknowledge. But she saw me. And that changed everything.

4

THE SACRED AGREEMENT

"We're all just walking each other home."
—Ram Dass

y wife has always been my greatest cheerleader. We met in college, and I still remember the first time I saw her. It was at an off-campus party, and I was standing between her boyfriend at the time and another friend of mine. As I scanned the backyard, my eyes locked onto a beautiful blonde in the sea of college students. Without thinking, I asked, "Who is that?"

"That's Brooks—my girlfriend," my friend replied as he walked toward her.

As he disappeared into the crowd, my other friend muttered under his breath, "That's my *future* girlfriend."

And in my mind, I said, *That's my future wife.*

The Moment That Changed Everything

Even though Brooks had a boyfriend, we became fast friends. We spent hours talking, laughing, and sharing about our lives. There was always something unspoken between us—an invisible thread pulling us together, even when life kept us apart.

After college, I moved to Chicago, then Los Angeles. Brooks was living in San Francisco, still dating my friend (the one who had called her his future girlfriend) off and on. She visited LA often, and every time she did, we'd spend time together. Those moments became the highlights of my month. I loved her. I wanted to be with her. But loyalty to my friend and fear of rejection kept me silent. Little did I know that she felt the same way.

Then one day, Brooks' sister called her and said, "You need to fly to LA tonight and tell Pete how you feel."

Brooks hesitated. "But what if he doesn't feel the same? What if I ruin everything?"

Her sister didn't waver. "If you don't do this, you'll regret it for the rest of your life."

That night, there was a knock at my door. When I opened it, there she was—her gorgeous smile stretching from ear to ear, but beneath it, something new. Her usual confidence was replaced by a quiet tremble, her energy buzzing with nervous excitement. She looked like a little girl standing on the edge of something big—equal parts exhilarated and terrified.

Before I could even process my surprise, she blurted out, "I have something to tell you."

I blinked, caught off guard but intrigued. "Go for it."

Her face softened, and her eyes locked onto mine. There was something different in them—something raw, something deeper than words. It was as if her soul had taken over, guiding her toward truth.

Then, as fast as she could get it out, she said, "I love you. I've always loved you, and I want to spend the rest of my life with you."

Her words hung in the air, her wide eyes shimmering with a mix of hope and fear. Her lips trembled between relief and dread, her breath catching as if she had just leaped off a cliff and was waiting to see if she'd fall or fly.

And in that moment, something beautiful shifted inside me. A warmth, a certainty, a love I had never felt before surged through me. A slow smile spread across my face, and I said, "I love you too, and I always have. And *I* want to spend the rest of *my* life with *you.*"

Our lips met, and it felt like coming home. That night, we stayed up talking about everything—our future, the number of kids we'd have, their names, where we'd live, the house we'd build, what we'd be like as old grandparents. It wasn't just the start of a relationship—it was the beginning of a life we had both been waiting for.

A Sacred Contract

A year later, at just twenty-five years old, I stood at the altar, my heart pounding as I watched my future wife walk toward me. She was the most beautiful woman I had ever seen, radiating a presence that felt both familiar and eternal. Our connection ran deeper than this lifetime—almost as if we had always known each other, always been destined to find our way back.

What I didn't know then was that this relationship would shape me in ways I couldn't yet comprehend. It would teach me the true meaning of love, surrender, and transformation. It would break me open and rebuild me. Looking back, I realize that without her, I wouldn't have become the man I am today.

She is my soulmate, and we were always meant to find each other. I believe that, like all soulmates, our souls made an agreement before we came into this world—to find one another and grow together in this lifetime. That is the essence of a soulmate—not just to love us but to awaken us. To challenge us, to reflect back to us the parts of ourselves we cannot yet see, and to strip away the illusions of who we think we are so we can remember who we've always been.

The Dharma of Relationships

What if the people we meet were written into our story long before we took our first breath? What if love, loss, heartbreak, and healing weren't detours—but the path itself?

The people we meet, the connections we forge, the love that finds us and refuses to let go—none of it is coincidence. Life is not random—it is deeply meaningful. I believe our souls brought us together with purpose, long before we even knew each other in this lifetime. It was as if, somewhere beyond time, a part of me had always been waiting for her, just as a part of her had always been searching for me.

When we stood on that altar and spoke our vows, we weren't just committing to love and companionship—we were stepping into something far greater. We were entering into a sacred agreement, a divine contract designed not just for our happiness but for our evolution. Love, at its highest level, is about transformation. It's about awakening parts of ourselves that would remain dormant if not for the reflection of another soul standing in front of us. That is the dharma of relationships—the spiritual purpose woven into our bond, the higher calling that pulls two people together in a way that defies logic or reason.

A true soulmate is more than someone who loves us unconditionally—they are someone who challenges us to grow, to see ourselves more clearly, to break down the illusions we hold about who we think we are. They push us toward the highest versions of ourselves, sometimes gently, sometimes forcefully.

Brooks and I were brought together for reasons beyond what either of us could have understood in the beginning. There have been moments in our marriage when I've resisted that growth—moments when I was confronted with truths I wasn't ready to accept. But through it all, she remained. And so did I. Loving each other. Believing in each other. Holding up a mirror so we could see beyond our own limitations.

Because that's the truth about sacred relationships: They don't affirm who you've become—they help you remember who you've always been.

The Real Work of Love

That initial spark—the rush of attraction that first draws you to your soulmate—is intoxicating. It's what makes love stories feel like fate, like magic, like something written in the stars. But as beautiful as that feeling is, it isn't what sustains a relationship. It's merely the invitation, the doorway into something deeper.

Because once the honeymoon phase fades—and it always does—what remains is the real work. The dharma your souls came together to fulfill. The sacred, often uncomfortable, often humbling work of learning how to love in a way that isn't about desire or excitement but about truth.

Real love isn't effortless. It isn't a fairytale. It doesn't stay easy or convenient, and it certainly doesn't always look like the highlight reels we see on social media. Real love is a mirror—it reflects back to us our deepest wounds, our unhealed insecurities, and the patterns we've spent a lifetime avoiding. It asks us to see ourselves honestly and to allow another to see us with the same clarity.

And if you embrace it—I mean truly embrace it—you'll discover that the work is far more interesting, far more attractive, and far more rewarding than the fleeting magic that first pulled you in. Because when the illusions fade, when the infatuation settles, you are left with the opportunity to do something far greater—to step into the transformation that your souls brought you together for.

To do that, you must go deeper.

When you strip away the layers of who you think you are—when you meet your partner in truth, and they meet you in truth—you step into a kind of love that demands your full presence. A love that requires more than just words, more than gestures, more than social media posts written to prove to the world—or even to your partner—that you care. Love isn't measured by how often you declare it online. It isn't in the carefully curated captions, the anniversary tributes, the over-the-top birthday messages meant for public consumption. Real love doesn't need to be exhibited.

It requires a willingness to be fully seen, in all your brilliance and all your brokenness, without hiding or performing. It requires an openness and vulnerability that will stretch you beyond your comfort, pushing you into the spaces you've spent a lifetime avoiding.

And it's there, in those uncomfortable places, that your deepest life lessons are waiting.

This is where the dharma of your relationship will be revealed—not in the easy moments, not in the passion of new love, but in the hard conversations, in the forgiveness that feels impossible, in the choice to stay open when every part of you wants to shut down.

Because love isn't just about being chosen. It's about choosing—again and again, every day, even when it's hard. Even when it would be easier to retreat into old habits, old fears, old wounds.

The real work of love isn't about keeping the spark alive. It's about letting it burn away everything that isn't real so that what remains is something unshakable, something enduring, something that neither time nor hardship can break.

The Mirror of Love

For me, that lesson came through Brooks.

Throughout our marriage, she has seen in me what I couldn't yet see in myself—pushing me, challenging me, loving me in a way that has cracked me open and forced me to grow. I have been so fortunate to have Brooks by my side. She has always believed in me—always told me I was brilliant, creative, capable of anything—and this faith in me forced me to confront a truth I had spent my entire life avoiding: that maybe I was more than the limitations I placed on myself. But before I could fully step into that truth, I would first have to face the man I had been running from all along.

*Celebrating Brooks' birthday in Punta Mita, Mexico (2020)—one of many
moments of joy, love, and gratitude.*

5

THE WAR WITHIN

"Until you make the unconscious conscious, it will direct your life and you will call it fate."
—Carl Jung

When I returned from Brazil, something unexpected happened. Instead of peace, I felt an unraveling. The voice in my head—the one that planned, pushed, and controlled—had always been there, but I had never questioned it. I thought it was *me*.

But once I became aware of it, I couldn't *not* see it. And now that voice was *all I could hear*.

It wasn't just background noise anymore. It was relentless. Constant. And no matter how much I wanted to tune it out, I couldn't.

The Universe Intervenes

Then, as if orchestrated by something beyond me, Brooks came home from the salon with a small white card in her hand.

"I met someone today," she said, handing it to me. "I think you should call her."

She told me how she had been getting her hair cut, talking to her stylist about my awakening in Brazil—how profound it had been, but also how much I had been struggling since coming back.

A woman in the chair next to her, a total stranger, had been listening. Eventually, she leaned over and said, "I'm sorry—I was totally eavesdropping. But your husband needs to call Michelle. She changed my life."

I looked down at the card and something inside me stirred. I was still in the afterglow of my experience in Brazil, still committed to surrender—but at the same time, I was struggling. The voices in my head had been relentless, pulling me back into old patterns of doubt and control. Yet, beneath the noise, I could feel it—the undeniable pull of an unseen force, one I was just beginning to trust.

The universe is always guiding us toward wholeness, nudging us in the direction of healing and truth. Sometimes, those signs are subtle—a gut feeling, a whisper of intuition. And sometimes, they grab you by the collar and shake you awake, leaving no room for doubt. This was one of those moments.

I didn't hesitate. I grabbed my phone and dialed the number.

Meeting Michelle

Two days later, I found myself sitting in Michelle Bronson's home. I didn't know who she was, what she did, or why I was even there. But something told me I was exactly where I needed to be.

Michelle was unlike anyone I had ever met. She carried this effortless cool, this deep, quiet knowing that radiated from her. She had an energy that made you feel comfortable, made you feel normal, made you feel like you could let down your guard and not be judged.

We began the session, and I told her everything—about Brazil, about the awareness that had been consuming me since I left the jungle. And then I told her about the voices—the constant internal dialogue, the never-ending push to plan, control, and analyze. It was as if that experience had unlocked a door I hadn't even known was there, and now, for the first time, I could hear them clearly.

And all I wanted was for them to be silent.

Holding a Balloon Underwater

She listened intently, a small smile forming at the corners of her lips, as if she had heard this story a thousand times before.

"Pete, we're not just one single self," she said. "We're made up of many different parts—each with its own role, its own voice, its own purpose. Some parts protect, some push, some analyze, some keep us safe. But when we ignore them, when we pretend they don't exist, they don't just disappear. They get louder."

She paused, then looked at me and said something that made me stop, caught between curiosity and confusion.

"Our goal isn't to quiet those voices. Our goal is to listen to them."

She leaned in. "The more you push them down, the more they'll fight to rise. Have you ever tried to hold a balloon underwater? The harder you push it down, the more resistance you feel—until eventually, it bursts to the surface with full force. That's what's happening inside of you. Those voices are parts of you that have been waiting to be heard for a very long time."

I sat there, trying to process what she was saying. I had spent my entire life trying to silence them.

But what if she was right?

What if I had been fighting a battle I was never meant to win?

The Man Arrives

Michelle handed me two small metal rods and told me to hold one in each hand. They began to vibrate in a rhythmic pattern, left to right, like a gentle pulse moving through me. She asked me to close my eyes, and then she began to speak—not to me but to one of the voices inside my head.

"The part of you that's always in control, the part of you that's in charge—can I speak to him?"

I wasn't sure who she was talking about. *I'm the one in charge,* I thought.

Sensing the confusion on my face, she asked, "The part of you that never lets you slow down, that keeps pushing no matter what—can he step forward?"

The moment she called him forward, I didn't just acknowledge him —I became him. My entire body shifted. My breath became slow, controlled. My spine straightened, my shoulders squared, my hands gripped the arms of the chair. My jaw tightened with certainty. My voice dropped, firm and measured. Every movement, every response was precise, deliberate. There was no hesitation, no room for uncertainty.

I wasn't just channeling this part of me—I was *fully embodying* him. The version of me that planned, controlled, and never wavered. The one who never let up, never loosened his grip. The one who had carried me this far.

The Man had arrived.

The Protector and the Fear of Failure

I could feel his strength. Solid. Unshakable. He had always been there, watching, waiting. The one who took over when things got hard. The one who never flinched, never broke.

And then Michelle asked him, "What would Pete be without you?"

Without hesitation, the words spilled out of my mouth. "He would be a complete and utter failure."

As I heard myself say it, something inside me cracked. The truth of those words hit me like a tidal wave. This was the part of me that had been driving me my entire life. The voice that told me I had to be perfect, that I had to keep striving, that I could never let my guard down.

This was the part that never let me cry in front of Brooks—the part that equated vulnerability with weakness, that kept me armored, always in control, always proving, always *holding it together.*

And then Michelle did something I wasn't expecting. She thanked him. She validated him. She told him how important he was, how much he had done for me.

The Man stood a little taller. I could feel his energy swell inside me, a quiet but powerful surge of pride. It was as if, for the first time, he was being seen—not as something to fight against but as something valuable. As if he had finally heard the words he had been waiting for his entire life.

Michelle leaned in, her voice calm but direct. "You've worked so hard to protect him. What is it you've been trying to keep him safe from?"

Without hesitation, The Man answered. "Failure. Weakness. Embarrassment. If I let my guard down, he'll lose everything."

Michelle nodded. "And what will happen if you stop pushing him so hard?"

There was a long pause. A heaviness settled over me. The Man's answer came slowly, measured. "He'll fall apart."

Michelle let his words settle in the air for a moment before asking, "And then what?"

The Man exhaled sharply, almost irritated by the question. "Then he'll be nothing. A failure. A disappointment. He'll prove everyone right—the ones who doubted him, the ones who never believed in him."

Michelle's voice remained steady. "And if that happens . . . what does it mean about *you*?"

The Man tensed. "It means I failed him."

"How long have you carried that responsibility?" she asked.

"As long as I can remember," he said without hesitation. "Since he was a kid. Since the first time I knew he was weak."

Michelle nodded slowly. "And who told you weakness was dangerous?"

The Man didn't answer right away. The energy inside me shifted—less certainty, more weight. When he finally spoke, his voice was lower, almost distant. "Everyone. The world. His teachers. Everyone thinks he's weak."

Michelle leaned in just a little closer. "And what would happen if, just for a moment, you stepped back?"

The Man stiffened again. "He wouldn't know what to do. He'd be lost. I'm the only reason he's alive."

Michelle thanked him again for all his hard work and asked if he would step aside for just a moment. She wanted to speak to another part of me but assured him he could come back soon. With hesitation, The Man agreed, and his energy left my awareness.

Enter The Exile

Michelle watched the shift in my body, her voice now softer, more gentle. She let the silence linger before asking, "Can I speak to the part of Pete that first felt weak?"

Instinctively, I felt something change. My knees pulled together, my shoulders hunched, my hands folded in my lap. My voice softened into something almost childlike. This part of me—The Exile, the part The Man had spent a lifetime protecting—was so small. So young. So sad.

I felt the sadness rising in my chest before I could stop it—before I even understood why it was there. A tightness, a pressure, a dam I hadn't even realized I had built over decades. My throat clenched. My breathing grew uneven. And then—before I could hold it back—the first tear slid down my face.

I tried to swallow it down. Tried to blink it away. But it was too late. The dam broke. And suddenly, I wasn't just crying—I was unraveling. Sobbing uncontrollably in front of another person. Each breath felt like a confession. Each tear a surrender to a vulnerability I couldn't contain.

A part of me panicked. What if she judged me? What if she saw me as weak? What if this—this display of raw emotion—meant I had lost control?

But Michelle didn't flinch. She didn't try to stop me. She didn't look away. She just sat there, present, holding space. And in that silence, something inside me shifted.

For the first time, I wasn't The Man holding everything together—I was the little boy who had carried it all for so long. And in that moment, I didn't just let him cry—I let him be seen. I let him be heard. I let him exist.

A Life Labeled Before It Even Began

Through tears, this little boy inside of me spoke, his voice barely more than a whisper. He told Michelle that when Pete was younger, the world had already decided who he was before he even had a chance to prove otherwise.

He was the bad kid. The troublemaker. The one who couldn't sit still, couldn't follow directions, couldn't do things the way the other kids did. The teachers didn't see potential in him—they saw a problem. And they made sure he knew it.

But that wasn't the only thing the world had decided about him. He was also the smallest. The weakest.

Puberty arrived late, as if his own body had left him behind, and by the time it finally came, he had already learned the painful truth—that if you don't get bigger, faster, or stronger, you better find another way to prove you belong.

And so, he did. He became the kid who could make people laugh, the one who pushed boundaries, who found ways to get attention, even if it meant getting in trouble. Because being seen—even for the wrong reasons—was better than not being seen at all.

His test scores told him he wasn't smart. His teachers told him he was difficult. That he would never amount to anything. They didn't say it with concern or care—they said it with frustration, with impatience, with exhaustion, as if he was too much for them to deal with. And eventually, he believed them.

School wasn't a place of learning for him—it was a battlefield. He felt like he was always in trouble, always being sent to the hallway, always the one getting called out. He wasn't given extra help or encouragement—he was given labels. And once those labels stuck, there was no peeling them off.

His teachers didn't just dislike him. They *hated* him. One of them even grabbed him by the collar, shoved him up against a wall, and threatened him.

The Teacher's Regret

And yet, decades later, that very teacher would return—haunted by what she had done.

When I was forty years old, my mother was at church when a woman hesitantly approached her.

"Are you Mrs. Kennedy?" she asked, her voice careful, uncertain.

My mother, slightly suspicious but curious, nodded. "Yes . . . ?"

Tears welled in the woman's eyes before she could even speak the next words.

"I was Peter's teacher in grade school."

She paused, the weight of it all pressing against her. My mother studied her face, waiting.

"I've been holding this for so many years," the woman said, her voice trembling. "I was a new teacher, and I didn't know how to handle a child like him." She swallowed hard, struggling to force the words out. "And . . . I mistreated your son. It has tortured me all these years."

Decades later, her regret still lived inside her. And though the apology came long after I had stopped expecting one, it didn't come too late to mean something.

But still, it didn't bring peace.

It didn't erase the years of sadness, the feeling of being cast aside before I even had a chance to prove myself. If anything, it made the little boy inside me rage. Rage at the teachers who had labeled him, at the adults who had failed him, at a world that had judged him before he even knew who he was. Because now I knew the truth—she had seen what she did.

Her tears didn't change the fact that I had spent a lifetime feeling like one of the bad people. That for years, I had believed them—that I was the problem, that I was broken, that I was defective.

And now, suddenly, she was unburdening herself, expecting . . . what? Forgiveness? Closure?

No. Not yet. Maybe not ever.

The little boy inside me didn't want her guilt. He wanted justice. He wanted to scream, to make her feel the pain she had caused. He wanted to rage, to fight back against the years of being silenced.

But he didn't.

All he had was silence.

And so, instead of fighting, he withdrew. He shrank. He carried a deep sadness, an unbearable loneliness, a quiet certainty that the world had already made up its mind about him—and that nothing he did would ever be enough to change it.

I sat there sobbing as this little boy inside me poured out a lifetime of pain. I had ignored him for so long, locked him away, convinced he wasn't worth listening to. But now, sitting in that chair, I felt nothing but deep empathy for him—like he was my own child—and the thought of him carrying this pain alone was unbearable. I would never let my own child feel this way. So why had I let *him*?

Meeting Him with Love

Through my tears, I whispered to him, "I'm so sorry. You were never bad. You were never broken. You were perfect." I could feel his sadness soften, just a little, as if someone had finally seen him.

Michelle smiled gently and spoke to him with the warmth of a mother comforting a child. She thanked him for sharing his pain, for carrying so much for so long. Then, in a voice filled with certainty, she assured him, "You are no longer alone. Pete is here now. He sees you. He loves you. And he's never going to leave you."

A deep stillness settled over me. The little boy inside of me—this Exile I had abandoned for so many years—was finally being welcomed home.

Then Michelle asked The Man to return.

The Man Returns

There was no hesitation—The Man was ready, as if he had been waiting. The moment he stepped forward, my body stiffened, my voice dropped, and my posture straightened. Control reclaimed its place.

And then she asked a simple question.

"What do you think about that little boy?"

Without hesitation, the words came out of my mouth, "I fucking hate that little pussy."

The force of those words stunned me. I had never consciously thought them before, but I felt the truth in them. The Man despised the boy. To him, that little boy was weak, pathetic—everything he had fought to protect me from becoming.

And yet, as soon as the words left my lips, something inside me recoiled. I had just spent the last few minutes holding that little boy's pain, seeing him for what he truly was—not weak, not pathetic, but *wounded*. And now, The Man—the part of me that had built my entire life—was tearing him down, just like the world had.

A war was raging inside me.

Yes, there was still a part of me that saw the boy the way The Man did. Vulnerability was dangerous. Tears meant weakness. Sadness was something to be buried, not felt. That was what I had always believed— what The Man believed. And because of that, I had spent my entire life unable to access my own pain, shutting down any emotions that threatened my strength. I could feel anger. I could feel drive. But sadness? Grief? Hopelessness? Those were things I had never allowed myself to feel.

That was *The Man's* doing.

At that moment, I saw him for what he really was. Not just my protector, not just the force that had built my success—but the very thing that had kept me from feeling. He had walled off my pain, buried my sadness, and in doing so, had stolen a part of me that I desperately wanted back.

The Battle Begins

A wave of disgust rose in me. Not toward the little boy this time, but toward *The Man*.

I quickly grew a deep disdain for him, seeing him now for what he truly was—the barrier between me and everything I had spent my life avoiding. He had kept me from feeling, from grieving, from ever allowing myself to be vulnerable. And for that, I resented him.

My battle with The Man had just begun.

6

THE ILLUSION OF DETACHMENT

"One does not become enlightened by imagining figures of light, but by making the darkness conscious."
—Carl Jung

After I became aware of The Man, I wanted nothing to do with that part of me. He was the enemy—the part of me that had built my prison of striving, perfectionism, and fear. The moment I saw him for what he was, I made a decision—I would do everything in my power to erase him. I would become his opposite. If The Man was control, I would be surrender. If The Man was ambition, I would be stillness. If The Man was power, I would be vulnerability.

Chasing Enlightenment Like Success

I turned to meditation like a drowning man grasping for air. I dove headfirst into the practice, convinced that if I sat long enough, breathed deeply enough, detached fully enough, I could transcend The Man. My goal wasn't just to quiet my mind—I wanted to obliterate the part of me that had ruled my life for decades.

At first, I treated meditation the way I treated everything else in life —like a mission to complete, a challenge to conquer. I approached it with the same drive I had once applied to building businesses, only now my competition wasn't in boardrooms or balance sheets—it was within me. How many hours could I sit before my body went numb? How far could I push my mind before it would break? I believed the path to enlightenment was one of hard work and resilience, so I meditated every day for as long as I had to.

But the more I tried to escape The Man, the more he persisted. The more I tried to silence him, the louder he became. I would sit in meditation, desperately trying to detach, and his voice would creep in:

"This is stupid. You're wasting time."

"You think you're spiritual now? You're such a fake."

I thought meditation would purify me, but instead, it became another battleground. And just like every battle I had fought within myself before, I was losing.

All the effort—the discipline, the hours logged in silence—only seemed to tighten the grip. Meditation didn't liberate me. It just exposed the war I was still waging inside.

Eventually, I started looking elsewhere.

The Retreats—Searching Beyond Myself

I went on retreat after retreat, traveling the world in search of discomfort and pain to erase The Man. Each one challenged me to my core— similar to the one in Brazil, but even more intense and more revealing— pushing me to confront the parts of myself I had spent a lifetime avoiding.

I was chasing my edge—seeking deeper experiences, more spaces that stripped me of distraction and forced me into the present moment. I believed enlightenment was something to attain, something I could reach through sheer force of will. The irony was lost on me at the time —I was chasing liberation with the same hunger I had once chased success. Different pursuit, same desperate energy.

Many of these retreats involved working with plant medicine—iboga, ayahuasca, and psilocybin. Each one unlocked a different layer of my psyche, peeling back defenses I didn't even know I had. These ceremonies weren't casual experiments—they were initiations. Deep, unpredictable, and often brutal mirrors.

They stripped everything away—food, comfort, sleep. Days stretched endlessly in silence. My mind opened. The deeper I went, the stranger it all became. Time ceased to exist. I found myself in spaces where the boundary between reality and something beyond it began to blur.

There were moments of euphoria, of profound clarity—times when I felt like I had unlocked some hidden truth of the universe. And then there were nights that dragged me into the depths of my fears, forcing me to confront my need for control in the most terrifying ways.

The experiences were otherworldly. Sometimes, I felt my body dissolve entirely, merging with the vast unknown. Other times, I was plunged into visions so vivid they felt more real than waking life—visions that stripped me of my identities, my attachments, my illusions of control. I would come face-to-face with parts of myself I had buried long ago, parts I didn't even know existed. And still, I pushed deeper, trying to dissolve The Man.

I convinced myself that this was the path to enlightenment. That this suffering was proof I was evolving. That if I could endure more than the others, if I could go further, I would somehow transcend my own humanity.

I was trying to break myself so I could break The Man.

The Illusion of Detachment

I didn't realize it at the time, but I had fallen into one of the greatest traps of the spiritual path—the illusion of detachment. It seduces you with the promise of freedom—freedom from suffering, from attachment, from the self you no longer wish to be. But in the pursuit of detachment, you can end up creating yet another identity, another mask to wear, another illusion to cling to.

I didn't see it at the time, but I had simply traded one prison for another. The Man had been obsessed with achievement, with control, with proving his worth through success. So I decided to be his opposite. I rejected everything he stood for—ambition, discipline, power. I told myself I didn't need to win, I didn't need to strive, I didn't need to be anything at all. I was above it. Beyond it. I had transcended.

But had I?

The trap of enlightenment is that it can become just another identity. And that's exactly what happened to me.

I started identifying as "the seeker". The one who had renounced their preferences. The one who had let go. The one who was above worldly attachment. And in doing so, I had built another illusion—another persona to hide behind.

I did what a seeker would do. I read so many books, listened to so many teachers. I chased wisdom like I had once chased wealth. I told myself I was on a different path now, but the truth was, it was the same damn path—I was just wearing a different disguise. I was still chasing. Still trying to become something.

But if I was truly free, why did I feel the need to prove it? Why did I cling so desperately to this new identity? Why did I secretly judge those who were still caught in the chase for success, as if I had somehow risen above them?

I had convinced myself that detachment meant erasing the past. That by abandoning my old self, I could be reborn into something pure, something enlightened. But real detachment isn't about erasing—it's about integrating. It's about seeing all parts of yourself with absolute clarity and accepting them rather than trying to destroy the ones that make you uncomfortable.

I had failed to see that my desire to become "the monk on the mountain" was just another form of striving. Another way to measure my worth. Another role to perfect.

True detachment isn't about escape—it's about meeting every part of yourself, including the ones you want to erase, with complete acceptance.

I wasn't ready to see that yet. But the realization was coming sooner than I could have imagined.

7

THE BODY REMEMBERS

"The body keeps the score."
—Bessel van der Kolk

My wife returned from a retreat in Costa Rica glowing with the kind of clarity that only comes from deep inner work. She told me about a woman she met there—a therapist named Concetta—someone she felt could guide me on my own journey. Another nudge from the universe. Another loving act of encouragement from our sacred agreement. Brooks and the universe were gently guiding me toward the person I was always meant to be.

Concetta had this peaceful aura about her—intuitive, connected to something deeper. She carried a reverence for life, for the process of transformation, and for the tools she had mastered to help people unlock their greatest potential. She was a body-based expressive therapist, meeting people where they were and guiding them back into embodiment—back to the radiance and life force they had abandoned.

The Body Remembers What the Mind Forgets

Concetta introduced me to a new term—*somatic therapy*.

Unlike traditional talk therapy, which focuses on thoughts and emotions, somatic therapy understands that trauma and unresolved experiences are stored in the body. It uses techniques like breathwork, movement, and mindfulness to help individuals access and release deeply held tension and emotional blockages. I had spent my life trying to think my way out of pain, searching for the right ideas, philosophies, or perspectives to fix myself. But what I didn't realize was that the key to unlocking my potential wasn't getting out of my mind—it was getting into my body.

My sessions with Concetta were forty-five-minute deep dives into my internal world. Eyes closed, I would scan my body for tension, fear, anxiety—places where emotions had taken root. Concetta would guide me, asking me to describe these sensations. The color. The texture. The shape. And then, she would have me speak to them. Ask them what they needed. And the responses were loud and clear.

The Power of Ownership

One of the first patterns Concetta helped me recognize was a subtle but profound habit—*pushing off my thoughts and feelings onto others so I didn't have to own them.*

I would say something like, "You know when you wake up and instantly have to jump out of bed, wake your kids up, and get them ready for school? How it can feel like you wake up in complete chaos?"

Concetta would pause. "Hmm . . . I don't actually—since I don't have children. But I'd love for you to try that again . . . and say it as your experience."

So I would. "When I wake up, I jump out of bed, wake up my kids, and get them ready for school. *I* feel like I wake up in complete chaos."

Wow. What a difference.

That simple shift—owning my thoughts and emotions instead of externalizing them—was a revelation. When you take full ownership of your feelings, they become something you can work with. Something you can change. Avoiding ownership, on the other hand, keeps you stuck, waiting for the world to shift instead of shifting yourself.

When you place responsibility for your emotions onto someone or something else—whether it's your spouse, your boss, your kids, or Mercury doing its retrograde thing again—you give away your power. You become reactive, waiting for external conditions to change so you can feel better. But when you own your emotions, you take back control. You recognize that the way you experience life isn't dictated by outside forces but by your own internal state. This shift isn't just about language—it's about empowerment. It means that if I feel chaos in my mornings, *I* have the ability to create a different experience. If I feel unfulfilled, *I* can explore why. If I feel disconnected, *I* can take action to reconnect. Ownership is the first step toward transformation—because you can't change what you refuse to claim as yours.

The Power of Language

Another pattern I hadn't noticed was how I used self-deprecating language to undercut my own emotions.

At one point during a session, I said, "I know it's stupid, but when my life feels out of control, I start to control whatever little things I can, like cleaning the kitchen."

Again, Concetta gently stopped me. "Nothing you do is stupid. Try saying that again without judgment."

So I did. "When my life feels out of control, I start to control whatever little things I can, like cleaning the kitchen."

Again—what a difference. By stripping away shame from my words, I was giving myself permission to *be*—to feel, to act, without undermining my own experience. It was a small shift, but it carried weight. Instead of dismissing my coping mechanisms as foolish or unnecessary, I was acknowledging them as valid responses to my internal state. I wasn't just changing my words—I was changing my relationship with myself.

Language is powerful. The way we speak to ourselves, the way we describe our experiences, shapes how we perceive them. When we minimize our emotions—when we label them as "stupid" or "ridiculous"—we deny ourselves the space to process them fully. But when we remove judgment, we make room for understanding. And understanding is the foundation of healing.

Concetta had this instinctual ability to see everything before it was clear to me. Up to this point, only a few people had that ability—the shaman in Brazil, Michelle, and now Concetta.

The Return of The Man

In my very first session with Concetta, as I scanned my body, I noticed a tightening on my right side—an energy that felt strong, angry, unrelenting. Concetta sensed it too. Without hesitation, she spoke to it.

"Wow," she said. "You're an important part of Pete's life. I mean, it sounds like you are *the man*!"

I froze. I had not told Concetta about *The Man*—the part of me I had been trying to escape, the part I wanted to divorce myself from.

And then, the voice inside me responded, "That's right. I am The Man."

Shit. He was back.

All it took was one phrase from Concetta, and boom—his energy consumed me. This was not what I was here to work on. I was here to grow, to evolve, to become "the monk on the mountain" and transcend my human flaws. But here I was again, slipping back into what I so desperately wanted to escape.

For days after that session, I wrestled with what had happened. I had spent so much time trying to push this part of me away, convinced that true transformation meant erasing him. But no matter how hard I tried, he was still there. The tension, the fire, the force of him—it wasn't fading. And if ignoring him hadn't worked before, it certainly wasn't working now.

I didn't have an answer yet, but something in me knew I had to keep going.

The Shift That Changed Everything

Over the next few months, going deep inside my body became easier. It became a path to crystal-clear insights and life lessons. I couldn't wait to work with Concetta each week because I was *learning*—learning more about myself than I ever had before.

One thing I've found in life is that I'm drawn to people who *have something I want*. Concetta had this air about her—confident, kind, intuitive, grounded. Every moment of her life seemed like a ceremony.

What does that mean? It means there is reverence in everything. Everything is a gift from the universe. She moved through life as if every moment held sacred significance. And I wanted that.

I told her, "You always seem so calm and steady. I keep finding myself getting frustrated. Then I get mad at myself for getting frustrated. Then I get mad at myself for getting mad at myself for getting frustrated."

She smiled. "I get frustrated all the time. You don't see that side of me because when we're together, I'm working. I'm holding space for you, and I hold my professionalism with absolute reverence. But outside of these sessions, I get mad and frustrated all the time. I just don't get mad at *myself* when I do."

Light bulb. Mind blown.

Once again, I had been trying to divorce myself from parts of me I didn't like instead of integrating them. I had spent so much time believing that true growth meant eliminating my flaws, when in reality, growth meant learning to hold them without shame.

I wasn't failing because I got angry—I was failing because I believed I *shouldn't* get angry. That was the real illusion—the idea that certain emotions made me weak, less evolved, or unworthy of peace. But anger, frustration, sadness—these weren't signs of failure. They were signs that I was human. And if I could learn to accept them rather than suppress them, I could actually begin to move through them.

Avoidance only strengthened their grip. But acknowledgment? That was where true freedom began.

This wasn't about achieving some unattainable state of constant calm. It was about integrating every part of me—the joy, the rage, the doubt, the strength—so I could live *more* fully, not less.

That shift changed everything.

The Truth I Didn't Want to Hear

Throughout our sessions, Concetta would bring in The Man's energy and let him speak. I still hated him. I wanted nothing to do with him. He was the one who had cut me off from vulnerability, who had removed crying from my emotional wheelhouse. The one who—because I couldn't be truly vulnerable in front of my wife, my best friend in life—left me feeling undesirable and unlovable.

And then, after a couple of months, Concetta said something that hit me like a bomb. "The Man is not something separate from you. The Man *is* you. And by hating The Man, you're hating yourself. You need to love The Man."

Love him? Love *the guy who fucked over the little boy inside me*? Love *the one who buried my softness in shame*? Love *the part of me that made me feel unworthy of love*?

As far as I was concerned, he could go fuck himself.

But Concetta wasn't wrong. I knew that my journey, just like everyone's, is a journey toward self-love, toward wholeness. I just wasn't ready. So she made a suggestion that sent a shock wave of fear through my body: "I think you're ready for a psilocybin ceremony."

8

THE MAN, THE BOY, AND ME

"Nothing ever goes away until it has taught us what we need to know."
—Pema Chödrön

To be clear, I hate psychedelics. While many people use them recreationally for fun, the only time I have used them is in ceremony for deep inner work. When you have a blindfold on, lying on a mattress after consuming a psychedelic, the journey is long and unpredictable, and any resistance can lead to the most challenging experience. As someone who struggled with control, resistance was often my experience, and what usually followed was what psychonauts describe as the Hell Realm.

The Hell Realm isn't a place—it's a state of being, a manifestation of our deepest fears, unresolved trauma, and the resistance to letting go. It's the mind desperately clawing for control in a space where control is an illusion. The more we fight it, the deeper we sink. Our own resistance becomes the architect of our suffering, turning discomfort into terror, fear into agony. It's a realm where time dissolves, and we are left alone with our darkest thoughts, amplified, inescapable, and relentless. The only way out is through surrender, but surrender, when you're trapped in the illusion of control, feels impossible.

But I trusted Concetta fully and knew that with her guidance, I could navigate the experience and surrender.

Preparing for the Ceremony

To prepare, we worked on my intention, which was clear as day—*get to know The Man*. Not love him. Not see his value. Just *get to know him*. Concetta also asked me to collect some photos from my past and bring them to the ceremony. Before we began, we would place them around the room to surround me with their essence.

A week before the ceremony, I met with Concetta, nervous but ready. I still believed at the time that true suffering was the path to salvation. When she asked to see the photos I planned to bring, I proudly showed her pictures of myself at different ages—times when I was happy, loved myself, and felt whole.

She studied them, then gently said, "These are all lovely, Pete. I'd love for you to bring one that truly represents your abundant self-love, but I also want you to look for the photos you've hidden away. The ones in the back of your closet. The ones that, when you see them, make you feel small, unlovable, undesirable."

Oh shit. *Those* photos?

The ones that proved I was weak? The ones that made me feel like I didn't belong? The ones I had buried because looking at them made me cringe with shame?

I went searching, and as I flipped through my past, I gathered the images of the version of me I had spent a lifetime rejecting.

A week later, I flew to meet Concetta for the ceremony, bringing only my eye mask and a stack of photos of myself that I hated.

Entering the Ceremony

Psychedelic ceremony is the ultimate Hero's Journey—a mythic arc that has played out in human consciousness for thousands of years. It's the call to adventure, the descent into the unknown, the battle with darkness, and the triumphant return with wisdom. When I stepped into my first ceremony in Brazil, it felt foreign, even absurd—why were these people singing to molten-hot grandmothers? Why did the rattles feel like they were vibrating in my chest? But over time, I realized that this was not just ritual for the sake of ritual—it was a gateway, a container for transformation.

What I once saw as strange has become sacred. Ceremony isn't about the external theatrics—it's about setting the stage for your own internal odyssey.

And psychedelics? They don't just hand you enlightenment. They rip you apart. They test you. They drag you through the underworld, forcing you to face your deepest fears, your buried pain, your illusions. That's why I hated them. They expose everything you don't want to see. They demand surrender. And surrender, when you've spent your whole life gripping on to control, is pure agony.

But what made me love ceremony—even though I still hated psychedelics—was what waited on the other side. The return.

In Joseph Campbell's *The Hero's Journey*, the hero doesn't just go on an adventure. He must descend into the abyss, face his greatest trials, die to his old self, and emerge reborn. That's what a psychedelic ceremony is. And when you make it through, when you conquer the Hell Realm, when you stare your fear in the face and refuse to run, you don't just survive—you level up.

Every time I came out of a ceremony, I felt like I had just been through a cosmic war zone and come back stronger. Another scar, another lesson, another notch on my belt of being a spiritual gangster. It sharpened me. It burned away my bullshit.

And so, despite my hatred for psychedelics, here I was—standing at the threshold, about to step into the unknown. The familiar scents of burning incense and sacred wood filled the air, the rhythmic pulse of the ceremony already weaving its spell. There was no turning back —only the path forward, into whatever the medicine had in store for me.

Concetta thanked the mushrooms for their wisdom and guidance, and Mother Earth for providing the medicine. She ceremonially handed me the mushrooms, which I placed in my mouth, chewed a few times, then swallowed. No turning back now. I placed the eye mask on and put noise-canceling earphones over my ears.

Immediately, the outside world disappeared. Darkness. Silence. I noticed how much sight and sound distract from the voices in our heads. When you remove them, you are left with nothing but yourself.

Concetta pressed play on her masterfully constructed playlist, and suddenly, my thoughts weren't just thoughts—they were sensations in my body. Fear and anxiety weren't just ideas—they were waves of energy rippling through my chest, tightening my throat, sending shivers down my spine.

Then, the medicine took hold—and suddenly, my mind was no longer my own. The sounds from the music were strange. Foreign. My thoughts turned into resistance. *Why am I just seeing weird geometric shapes? I hate this music. What the fuck am I doing? Who am I? Why am I asking who I am? That's such a weird question. Oh fuck, this is going to suck.*

I tore off my headset and eye mask and sat up. The room was blurry. Concetta's face swirled like Van Gogh's *Starry Night*.

"This sucks," I told her. "I hate this music. I can't even think about my intention. What the fuck."

She nodded, unshaken, her presence unwavering. Her eyes, half-lidded, looked as if she were deep in a trance herself—completely attuned to the space, the energy, the unfolding of the ceremony. She wasn't reacting to my distress, wasn't trying to fix it. She was simply *there*, holding steady like an anchor in the storm. "Sit across from me."

I sat on the floor and crossed my legs in lotus position, grounding myself in the ancient posture of stillness and surrender. The floor beneath me felt both impossibly solid and strangely distant, as if I were caught between worlds—the familiar and the unknown, the controlled and the chaotic. My breath was shallow, my mind still racing, but Concetta's presence was steady, an unshakable force guiding me deeper into the moment. She guided me into meditation, into my breath, into my body. And within moments, I was *home*. Out of my mind and into my body. This was where my work was. I put my mask and headphones back on and sank in.

I recalled my intention. I called out to The Man.

"All right, dude. I'm here for you. I took these mushrooms to connect with you. Let's go. What do you have to say?"

His response was immediate and unsurprising.

The Return of The Man

He didn't appear as a person. He was a solid, metal, shiny ball, about the size of a basketball. And he zipped to the farthest corner of my mind, trying to be as far away from me as possible.

Then he spoke.

"What the fuck are you doing? Taking fucking mushrooms? You are *out of control!*"

I could hear the fear in his voice. "I want nothing to do with this. I'm buried in the middle of this metal ball. I can't feel anything, and I *definitely* can't feel those mushrooms. Enjoy your trip, you fucking idiot."

Well, shit.

I wasn't shocked by his reaction. It made sense. He *was* my control. And I was threatening his entire existence.

"All right, man," I said. "If you get bored or want to come down and hang, I'll be here."

And then, something else started happening.

The Purge

A deep yawn took over my body. Then another. And another. My mouth stretched wide, uncontrollable yawns pouring out of me for what felt like *thirty minutes straight*. It wasn't tiredness—it was *release*.

Then came the contractions. It started as a flicker—a subtle, almost imperceptible tightening in my core. Then, like a wave gathering force in the deep ocean, it surged through me, gripping my abs, my solar plexus, my shoulders in a relentless clench. My body was no longer under my command. I lifted off the ground, spine arched, breath held hostage, mouth stretched open in a silent exhale, as if something deep inside me was trying to break free.

Each time I thought it was over, another surge came—deeper,

stronger, more primal. My muscles locked in place, trembling from the sheer force of the energy moving through me. The tension wasn't just physical—it was something else—a force, an intelligence, something ancient that had been trapped inside me for years, maybe lifetimes. It felt like my body was fighting to expel something that had overstayed its welcome, something that had burrowed so deep into my being that I had mistaken it for *me*.

It hurt—a deep, raw, aching pain, not just in my muscles but in my very existence. And yet, beneath the discomfort, there was something else. Euphoria. A strange, intoxicating lightness threaded through the pain, as if each contraction was pulling me closer to liberation. I could feel the *release*, the unburdening, the uncoiling of something that had been wound too tight for too long.

I didn't need to understand it to know—this was my body purging. The area of my solar plexus—the very center of my personal power, control, and confidence—was finally releasing the years of trapped energy that had kept The Man locked away. The rigid walls that had once encased him, the armor I had built around my emotions, the tension I had carried since childhood—it was all being shaken loose, one contraction at a time.

It wasn't just my muscles convulsing—it was a reckoning. A breaking down of the structures that had ruled me for so long. A surrender, not to weakness but to the raw, untamed power that had been buried within me all along.

And then, as the final contraction passed, The Man came down from the wall. The ball transformed into *me*. And we lay there, shoulder to shoulder.

And then the next wave of purging hit—*rageful screaming*.

The Scream of a Lifetime

Anger flowed out of me like a dam that had suddenly burst. It was raw, uncontainable—decades of suppressed rage surging through me in violent waves. My body convulsed with the force of it, my hands clenching, my jaw tightening, my breath ragged and uneven. My chest burned with the pressure, my throat tightening like a vice, as if it had been holding back this scream for decades.

I felt a pillow being placed in my hands. Concetta. Even in the chaos, she was there. Instinctively, I gripped it, pulled it close, and pressed my face into the fabric. And then—I let go.

A primal, guttural scream ripped through me. Not a cry. Not a yell. A scream from the very depths of my being, from places inside me I had long since abandoned. It was pain. It was grief. It was rage. It was the voice of the boy who had been silenced, the boy who had been told he was too much, the boy who had been misunderstood, rejected, and cast aside. He had waited so long to be heard. And now, he was screaming.

But it wasn't just him.

The Man was there, too.

I could feel him beside me—not separate from me, but as real and alive as I was. He was screaming, crying, his rage merging with mine. And suddenly, we weren't in the ceremony anymore.

We were being pulled back—back through time, back through memory, back through every moment where we had been abandoned, unloved, unseen.

We were eight years old, lying in my childhood bed at night, screaming into the darkness, punching the pillow, thrashing under the weight of a pain too big for a child to hold.

We were ten, sitting alone in the hallway at school, sent out of class again, fists clenched, head down, pretending we didn't care—but we did.

We were twelve, standing in front of the mirror, staring at our reflection, wishing—begging—to be someone else.

We were fifteen, sixteen, seventeen, finding ways to prove we were strong, that we didn't need anyone, that we were fine.

We were raging at the world. At our teachers. At the people who had dismissed us, misunderstood us, who had made us believe we were broken.

But suddenly, I saw the truth.

We weren't screaming at them.

We were screaming at ourselves.

For creating The Man.

For believing the world hated us when, in reality, we had been the ones who rejected ourselves.

For spending a lifetime trying to be something—someone—we were never meant to be.

The realization cut through me like a blade, slicing through the illusion I had clung to for so long. It wasn't the world that had made me suffer. It was me. I had exiled the boy inside me, pushed him away, silenced his cries. And now, he and The Man were side by side, screaming together, releasing the grief, the anger, the betrayal.

The rage had nowhere left to go.

It burned itself out, the screams tapering off into deep, shuddering breaths. And then, in an instant, it stopped.

Silence.

Stillness.

A profound, indescribable peace settled over me.

The Reunion

I wasn't separate from The Man anymore.

I wasn't separate from the boy.

I was whole.

I lay there, completely drained, my body sinking into the mattress beneath me as if I had just returned from battle. It wasn't just exhaustion—it was the weight of a lifetime finally lifted, the remnants of war dissolving into the stillness around me. I had walked through the fire, faced the darkness, fought the demons that had lived inside me for as long as I could remember. I had screamed, raged, surrendered, and emerged on the other side.

I had just run the Hero's Journey.

And I had won.

I turned inward, expecting to feel empty, hollow from the release. But instead, I felt something else—something unexpected.

Love.

Not just for the boy who had carried the wounds.

Not just for The Man who had carried the weight.

For both of them.

For all of me.

I loved The Man. I loved me.

The Final Test

I thought the ceremony was over, but the medicine had one final test. The whisper came, quiet but unmistakable.

"Do you love yourself?"

I laughed. "Yes."

And then, one by one, the photos appeared. The ones I had brought to the ceremony. The ones I had hated. The ones that once made me cringe, made me feel small, unworthy, unlovable.

My eighth-grade graduation photo. Bowtie. Fake glasses. A kid trying so hard to look smart, to look like he belonged.

I laughed. "Of course I love that little dude."

Then, my grade school football team picture. Giant shoulder pads. Tiny frame. A kid trying so hard to look big.

I laughed again, shaking my head. "That dude is awesome."

Every image, every version of me that I had rejected, suddenly looked perfect. Not because they had changed—but because *I* had.

And with that, the ceremony was over. The Man was no longer my enemy. The boy was no longer abandoned.

I was whole.

9

THE HAMSTER WHEEL

"Step into the fire of self-discovery. This fire will not burn you, it will only burn what you are not."
—Mooji

The first step to waking up is realizing you're on a hamster wheel. For most of my life, I didn't see it. I believed that if I just worked hard enough, achieved enough, and became enough, I would finally arrive at a place where I could rest. A place where I would feel at peace.

But the moment I got everything I had worked for, I realized the truth—there is no arrival.

In psychology, there's a concept called *The Arrival Fallacy*, a term coined by Dr. Tal Ben-Shahar, a Harvard professor specializing in happiness studies. It's the false belief that when we finally "arrive" at a goal—whether it's wealth, success, recognition, or even enlightenment—we will feel complete.

But that moment never comes. Because *The Arrival Fallacy* is just a hamster wheel disguised as a destination. You run and run, convinced that once you reach this milestone, this level of success, this personal breakthrough, you'll finally be free. But the moment you get there, you realize . . . the wheel hasn't stopped. It's just changed shape.

And here's the kicker—you're not just on one hamster wheel. You're on multiple wheels at the same time:

- **The career hamster wheel:** Every promotion, every deal, every milestone just resets the bar for what's next.
- **The personal growth hamster wheel:** You heal, transform, "do the work"—but the deeper you go, the more there is to uncover.
- **The relationship hamster wheel:** You find someone, fall in love—but when it gets hard, you wonder if someone else might make you happier.
- **The financial hamster wheel:** You think that once you hit a certain income or net worth, you'll finally feel safe—but the number always changes.
- **And it doesn't stop there.** There's a hamster wheel for everything—status, perfection, validation, even spirituality. No matter where you turn, there's another cycle pulling you in, convincing you that just *one more thing* will finally set you free.

We spend our lives running on these wheels. But no matter what milestone we reach, the moment we get there, we realize—we're still running. The only thing that's changed is the scenery.

And the truth is, there is no final destination.

Even when you get off one hamster wheel, you realize you're on another one. It's like climbing a mountain, believing that once you reach the peak, you'll be able to rest—only to see another mountain rising in the distance. And another. And another.

So what do you do once you see the hamster wheel?

Most people double down—run faster, push harder, chase the next fix. But there's another option—*stop running.* Look around. Take ownership of where you are.

Taking Ownership

Here's the hard truth: No one else is responsible for your happiness. Not your parents. Not your partner. Not your boss. Not society. Not the people who hurt you.

For most of my life, I didn't see this. I blamed circumstances. I blamed other people. I believed that if only they changed, if only things were different, then I'd finally be happy.

But that's just another hamster wheel—one where you run endlessly, waiting for the world to fix what only you can heal.

Taking ownership doesn't mean ignoring your pain or pretending your challenges weren't real. It means realizing that no one is doing anything *to* you.

They are simply doing their problem.

This was one of the most profound lessons I ever learned. I credit it to Greg Lawrence, a coach and mentor I worked with during one of the most challenging years of my life—when I was selling my company, Tagger Media, to Sprout Social (SPT: NASDAQ).

Greg helped me see that in every negotiation, each person—buyers, sellers, lawyers, investors—wasn't just making rational and irrational business decisions. Their decisions were shaped by far more than financial projections or contractual obligations. Their childhood experiences, fears, insecurities, personal ambitions, and deep-seated patterns were all at play, whether they realized it or not.

The investor pushing for more favorable terms at the last second? He had likely been burned in the past and was trying to make sure he never felt that kind of failure again. The buyer hesitant to commit? Maybe it wasn't just about risk management—maybe they had a life-long fear of making the wrong decision and letting people down. Even our own employees, the ones dragging their feet on due diligence deliverables, weren't just being slow or careless. Some of them were terrified of what the sale meant for their future—fearful of job security, nervous about change, or simply overwhelmed by the weight of an acquisition process they had never experienced before.

Once I understood this, negotiations stopped feeling like a battlefield and started feeling more like a psychology lab. I began to see the patterns beneath the surface. I stopped taking things so personally because I realized—it was never really about me. It was about them. Their programming. Their past experiences. Their subconscious fears and unspoken motivations.

And once I saw that, I couldn't unsee it. It changed how I approached every conversation, every decision, every difficult moment. It gave me the ability to pause, to step back, to ask, *What is really driving this person right now?* Instead of reacting emotionally, I could see the deeper layers of what was happening, which ultimately made me a better negotiator, a better leader, and a better human.

Because when you recognize that everyone is just "doing their problem"—playing out the scripts they've been subconsciously running their whole lives—you stop making their actions about you. And in that space, you gain the clarity and power to navigate even the most complex negotiations with wisdom, patience, and understanding.

That doesn't mean I don't react. Reacting is inevitable. It's part of being human. But the difference now is that I don't let my reactions drive the car—I see them as signals, as opportunities to course-correct.

I still get frustrated when someone cuts me off driving on a Los Angeles freeway. My initial instinct is to lay on the horn and give them the middle finger. But now, I catch myself. I pause. I recognize that my reaction isn't about them cutting me off—it's about my old fear of being undervalued, of having to fight for my space, to prove that I matter. It's not really about the guy in the other car—it's about the part of me that still believes respect has to be earned through dominance, through being seen, through not letting anyone take advantage of me.

The reality is, that person isn't out to disrespect me. They're probably not even thinking about me at all. Maybe they're having a terrible day—rushing to the hospital, late to an important interview, or distracted by the weight of losing someone they love. Or maybe they're stuck on their own hamster wheel, overwhelmed, blaming the world for their unhappiness, feeling unseen, unloved, and frustrated with life.

Whatever the reason, their actions have nothing to do with me. They're not a personal attack. They're just a reflection of whatever storm they're caught in at that moment. And when I see it that way, something shifts. My reaction softens. The anger dissolves. Because I know what it feels like to be lost in my own struggle, to be so consumed by my own stress that I become blind to the impact I have on others.

So instead of letting the moment fuel my old patterns—the need to be seen, to defend my space, to assert my worth—I take a breath and let it go. Because I see the truth—we're all just doing our problem. And the more compassion I have for others, the more compassion I can have for myself.

I don't always get it right. But the difference now is that I don't judge myself for reacting. I don't beat myself up or spiral into frustration. Instead, I see it as a street sign, flashing, *Hey, look over here. There's something deeper at play. Pay attention.* Because that's all a reaction really is—a marker, pointing to something deeper. And if you follow the signs, they'll lead you straight to the unhealed parts of yourself that still need attention.

It shifted my entire approach—not just in business but in life. I stopped assuming bad intentions. I stopped reacting from a place of victimhood. Instead, I started asking better questions:

- What unconscious fears or wounds might be driving this person's behavior?
- How can I separate their actions from my personal story?
- Where am I doing the same thing in my life?

Because once you recognize that everyone around you is just "doing their problem," the next level of awareness is realizing—*so are you.*

I had spent years running my own subconscious programs—chasing success, seeking validation, operating from old wounds I hadn't even acknowledged. Just like the lawyers, the investors, the buyers, the shareholders in that room, I was acting out my own conditioning too.

This is what taking ownership really means.

It's not just about recognizing your patterns—it's about seeing how those patterns shape the way you interpret the world around you. Because what you perceive as "problems" caused by others are often just reflections of your own unresolved wounds. And if you don't take ownership of them, you'll keep running on the hamster wheel—

repeating the same emotional cycles, blaming the same external forces, and wondering why you still feel stuck.

Breaking Free—Choosing Awareness Over Blame

Once you see this clearly, you gain an entirely new level of freedom. Because when you stop blaming others, you take back your power. You stop waiting for people to change, for circumstances to shift, for external validation to finally arrive.

Instead, you look within. You ask:

- What am I still holding on to?
- What belief is keeping me stuck?
- What parts of me need healing?

And then, the most important question of all: *What would happen if I finally stepped off the hamster wheel?*

Just by asking that question, you acknowledge something profound —there is a reality where the problem doesn't exist. The moment you entertain the idea that you could step off the wheel, that you could exist outside of it, that you could operate from a different level of awareness —you crack open the door to an entirely new way of being.

That's the shift. That's the moment the illusion starts to break. Because if there's a reality where this problem doesn't exist . . . why are you still running?

I didn't ask myself that question until I had already spent years running full-speed on the hamster wheel, convinced I was in control, chasing a dream I thought would set me free.

What I didn't see was that the chase itself was the thing trapping me. And nowhere was that more true than with Tagger.

10

THE COST OF THE CHASE

"Be careful what you set your heart upon—for it will surely be yours."
—James Baldwin

The thing about hamster wheels is that they don't just make you run in circles—they make you run faster. They convince you that if you just push harder, hustle longer, sacrifice more, you'll eventually break through. That there's a finish line out there somewhere.

I spent nine years running full speed on the Tagger hamster wheel. At the time, I didn't see it. I thought I was *building* something. *Chasing* success. *Providing* for my family. *Living* my purpose.

I thought I was in control.

But looking back now, I wasn't running toward anything. I was running *from* something.

And the faster I ran, the more I lost myself.

The Dream That Started It All

We started Tagger in 2015 with a simple but powerful idea—use social media to predict which musicians would blow up before they were signed. The concept made sense—if the most influential people in the music industry were all talking about a particular artist, chances were that artist was on the verge of breaking out.

But while the concept was simple, the execution was anything but.

At the time, our primary data source was Twitter's massive firehose of information. We didn't have access to all of Twitter's data—nor could we store it—so we had to be strategic about what we collected.

The first step was identifying who actually *mattered* in the music industry. We spent two months building a database of the most important people in the space—label executives, A&Rs, producers, music journalists, tastemakers—each with their corresponding Twitter handles. Once we had our list, we started collecting and analyzing their tweets in real time.

Then we ran into another challenge: We could see when someone influential mentioned a Twitter handle—@ShawnMendes, for example —but we had no idea who that person was. Were they talking about an emerging artist? A friend? A random account?

To solve this, we needed a second layer of intelligence—an automated way to predict whether a given Twitter handle belonged to a musician. The answer was hidden in Twitter bios. We built a system that scanned for key phrases like *new album, out now, singer-songwriter—*anything that suggested they were an artist.

Once both databases were up and running, we flipped the switch on our platform.

The results were *insane.*

Artists like Billie Eilish, Martin Garrix, and Lil Yachty surfaced on our platform before they had record deals. We watched in real time as their buzz grew, spreading from producers to label executives to music journalists. The platform was doing exactly what we had hoped—spotting the next big thing before the mainstream even knew they existed.

That's when it hit us. We weren't just analyzing social media chatter

—we were mapping influence. Predicting trends. Identifying the future of the industry before it happened.

We had something powerful—technology with undeniable potential.

But I had no clue what business could actually use it.

The Pivot

The music industry was the obvious choice. After all, we had built a system that could predict which artists would blow up before they were signed. Labels, managers, and A&R teams should have been banging down our door.

But we quickly realized a harsh truth—a handful of major labels controlled everything, and budgets were tight. Even if they loved what we built, the decision-making was slow, the competition for attention was fierce, and at the end of the day, there were only a *few* players who could actually pay for it.

We needed a market with *volume*—not just a handful of potential buyers but *thousands*. A space where influence mattered, where early insights could drive real revenue. We had the technology. Now we had to find the right industry to own it.

So we did the only thing that made sense. We got on a plane to New York City, the epicenter of business, and took every meeting we could get. Brands, advertising agencies, record companies, investors—anyone willing to sit across from us, I pitched to.

Accompanying me on this trip was my cousin and best friend, Dick Hillenbrand. He wasn't just a Tagger investor and board member—he was the person I turned to for guidance in life, for business decisions, and for the kind of unwavering support you only find once in a lifetime.

We have always had this bond—an unspoken understanding that no matter what, we had each other's backs. He was the one person I could tell my deepest secrets to and never feel judged. If one of us won, we both won. If one of us struggled, we carried the weight together. There was never competition, never resentment—just pure belief in each other's success and happiness.

Having him with me in New York wasn't just about business. It was about sharing the journey with someone who had been there from the very beginning, someone who knew what this moment meant. And I needed that support—because these meetings weren't going the way I had hoped.

I wasn't pitching just one idea—I was tailoring my pitch to every single person, hoping that at least one of them would light up and say, "Yes, this is it!"

But the yes never came. Not even close.

Most people listened politely, nodded, and gave vague responses before sending us on our way. Others looked at me like I was speaking a different language. And then there was one guy—an executive at a music company—who didn't just reject me. He yelled at me. He accused me of trying to rip off musical artists, of exploiting their work for profit. Coming from a record executive, there had to be some irony in that.

I walked out of that meeting shaken but not surprised. This was the game. We were throwing ideas at the wall, hoping something would stick. And so far, nothing had.

I was beginning to see the potentially fatal flaw in our approach. Many entrepreneurs build a product based on a cool idea—not on what the market actually needs. It's a common trap—falling in love with a concept and then scrambling to find a customer for it, rather than starting with a real problem and building a solution around it. It's like trying to force a round peg into a square hole or searching for a needle in a haystack when you don't even know if the needle exists.

It's an easy mistake to make, especially when you *believe* in what you've built. You convince yourself that if you just pitch it to the right person, in the right way, with the right angle, someone will see the vision and say *yes*. But that's not how business works. The best companies don't just create—they *solve*. And I was starting to realize that we hadn't yet figured out what we were actually solving.

I was already looking up earlier flights back to LA. New York had not been kind to us, and it was becoming painfully clear that we needed to go back to the drawing board on our strategy.

And then, as if by sheer intervention from the universe, one of our advisors called and said Gary Vaynerchuk's ("Gary Vee") team at VaynerMedia was open to meeting.

At the time, VaynerMedia was one of the fastest-growing advertising agencies, founded just six years earlier in 2009. But unlike traditional agencies, VaynerMedia had built its empire on social media at a time when most brands were still just dipping their toes in the water. Facebook had only started allowing ads on its platform two years before Gary launched his agency, and while the rest of the industry was still clinging to TV commercials and banner ads, VaynerMedia was helping brands actually connect with audiences where they were spending their time—on Facebook, Twitter, and YouTube.

Gary Vee was a social media phenomenon. He did more than simply understand these platforms—he anticipated where they were headed. He saw the future before others did, and the biggest brands in the world wanted his help to figure out how to reach consumers before social media became completely saturated with advertising.

His team was sharp. They were strategic. They were in demand by the biggest brands on the planet. And they knew it.

This was not going to be an easy meeting.

The Turning Point

When I walked into VaynerMedia's New York City office at Hudson Yards, it felt like stepping into a subway station at rush hour. The energy was electric—fast-paced, chaotic, and buzzing with intensity. They were growing so rapidly that people were literally sitting on the hallway floors, working on their laptops, crammed into every available space.

Vayner was *the* place to work. Gary Vee was an icon, and being part of his agency wasn't just a job—it was a badge of honor. But what struck me most wasn't the hustle. It was how young everyone was—I was easily fifteen years older than the oldest person I could see. The place was overflowing with raw energy, a relentless pace that felt border-line chaotic.

It looked like pure madness.

And I absolutely loved it.

I was shuffled into a small office that looked more like a dorm room than an executive's office. Jeff Nicholson, Senior Vice President of Paid

Media, was sitting on his couch, typing away on his laptop. Without looking up, he said, "What do you got?"

No small talk. No getting-to-know-you pleasantries. Just straight to the point.

In that moment, I realized something important—I was one of hundreds of vendors Jeff vetted monthly. VaynerMedia was looking for the best technology to fuel their agency's growth, and every tech vendor in the world wanted to sit in that chair. If I didn't grab his attention in the next five minutes, I'd be walking out of that office the same way I came in—just another pitch in a sea of forgotten demos.

I launched into my presentation, moving fast, knowing I had almost no time to make an impression. About three minutes in, Jeff suddenly held up his hand. "Hold on, Pete." He picked up his phone and, when someone answered, said, "Chris, can you come in here for a minute? I want you to see something."

Okay . . . Clearly, something in our platform had caught his attention. But what? And more importantly, who was Chris?

While we waited, Jeff softened. We started chatting about kids, life, things outside of work. It was a small shift but a meaningful one—I wasn't just another vendor anymore.

Chris Gesualdi, Director of Paid Media, walked in, shook my hand, and, in the deepest, most booming voice, said, "I'm Chris. Nice to meet you."

Chris, like Jeff, was all business. But Chris had a friendly curiosity about him. We jumped back into the demo, and every five seconds, Chris interrupted with a question. Not just surface-level questions—he wanted to understand the mechanics of the platform.

How reliable is this data?

How much can you capture?

How much can you store?

How much can we customize?

My answer was the same every time: "Whatever you want."

After grilling me on every possible detail, Jeff finally said, "Listen, we like your data. We like how you understand audiences on social media. But we need a platform that integrates that data into a workflow to run influencer marketing campaigns."

You need a what? I thought to myself. Influencer who?

I had no idea what he was talking about. I caught phrases like "we like your data" and "how you understand audiences on social media"—the rest was a different language.

So, I asked the only logical question, "What?"

They exchanged a look—part curiosity, part impatience, part disbelief—before Chris explained, "Influencer marketing is when brands pay people with big followings to promote their products on social media. We run influencer campaigns for brands all over the world, but we're managing that workflow and all the data in Excel. It's inefficient, slow, and prone to human error."

Bingo.

At last, someone wasn't just giving me a polite nod—they were telling me exactly what they needed. A real problem. A clear gap in the market. And, apparently, no one had built the solution yet.

Without knowing how—or even if—we could actually build it, I said, "We can absolutely build that solution for you."

Jeff leaned back. "Sounds good. If you can build it in a month, we'll be your first customer."

A month?

That sounded impossible. But that was all I needed to hear.

The Deep Dive

That night, I flew back to LA, packed a bag for a month, and moved into VaynerMedia's office. I was all in. I needed to learn every detail of how they operated—their workflow, data needs, inefficiencies—so we could build exactly what they needed.

Once again, Brooks was my biggest cheerleader. No "How long will you be gone?" No "Why do you have to live in their office?" She just gave me that proud, knowing look and said, "Go do it."

And I did.

A week at VaynerMedia, then a flight to Kraków, Poland, to work with our development team, then back to New York, then back to Kraków. It was a nonstop loop of learning, building, testing, and refining. I was obsessed—driven by the challenge of creating something new at breakneck speed.

And the energy at VaynerMedia? It was intoxicating. I wasn't just observing anymore—I was part of the team. Their fast-paced, sink-or-swim culture made me sharper. I absorbed everything I could.

And Chris? That wasn't the last time we worked together. His sharp mind, relentless curiosity, and attention to detail stood out from the very first meeting. Over the next two years, as he climbed the ranks to Vice President of Influencer Marketing at VaynerMedia, we would continue to collaborate closely. He became instrumental in shaping our product, providing insights that pushed us to refine and evolve Tagger in ways I hadn't even considered.

So when it came time to hire someone to lead product, the choice was obvious—I brought Chris on as Head of Product at Tagger.

The Moment of Truth

Exactly one month after committing to building their workflow into Tagger's platform, I stood in front of VaynerMedia's executive team, ready to present the finished product.

I had poured everything into this—sleepless nights, relentless flights between New York and Kraków, the weight of knowing that if this failed, there was no backup plan. No safety net. Our team worked tirelessly to hit the deadline.

But as I was about to walk into the meeting, a sudden wave of panic hit me.

How much was I going to charge for this?

In all the chaos of building, testing, and refining, I hadn't once stopped to think about pricing.

I stepped into the hallway, grabbed my phone, and called Daniel Savage, our Head of Business Development. Daniel was a salesman through and through—one of the best I had ever met. He had an instinct for deals, a sixth sense for reading a room, and a confidence that made closing feel effortless. He just knew how to sell. And throughout the Tagger journey, I learned more from him than I ever expected.

The second he picked up, I blurted out, "I need to give them a price. What do you think?"

Daniel didn't even pause. "$10,000 per month should work."

"$10,000? A month?" I repeated, almost laughing. "That's $120,000 a year. There's no way this is worth that. Plus, we're going to sell the same platform to every other brand and agency. Who in their right mind would pay that?"

Daniel was unfazed. "Pete, we just built exactly what they need. If they tried to build it themselves, it would cost them ten times that—if they could even pull it off."

I trusted Daniel, but I hadn't yet built the confidence to name a price that might offend a potential client. I was still learning that in business, hesitation can be the difference between winning and losing. Daniel had no such hesitation. He lived by a simple rule:

"If they don't throw up at your number, your price is too low."

I took a deep breath, walked back into the room, and presented the platform we had built for them. I walked them through every feature, every insight, every workflow we had tailored to their needs. I saw their eyes light up, their heads nodding in approval—we had exceeded their expectations.

And then it was time to deliver the price.

With as much confidence as I could fake, I said, "And it's $10,000 per month."

Silence. A brief moment where I braced for pushback.

But without hesitation, they agreed.

Tagger had its first customer.

Scaling Beyond the Startup Phase

And from there, we were off.

Sales and product development became my entire world. I thrived on the creativity of building something from nothing—the problem-solving, the constant iteration, the thrill of seeing an idea turn into a real, working product.

And I loved the energy of sales. Walking into a room, standing in front of a group of executives, and watching their eyes light up as I walked them through our platform—it was a rush every single time.

The hardest part wasn't selling the product. The hardest part was getting the meeting.

Finding the right person at a brand or agency—the one with the authority to say yes—was like fishing in a lake without knowing where the fish were. We chased leads, networked through connections, cold-emailed decision-makers. But once we got in the room, the hard part was over.

Because people were blown away by what we had built.

And I made sure they knew who else was using it.

I dropped the VaynerMedia name in every single pitch. Not as a sales gimmick but because VaynerMedia wasn't just any client—they were the leaders in the influencer marketing space. If they had bet on us, it meant we weren't just another startup with a flashy demo. We were the real deal.

And it worked.

Meeting by meeting, deal by deal, Tagger was becoming something real.

Every closed deal was more than just revenue—it was proof that we had created something indispensable. Each new client wasn't just another logo on the website—it was a signal that what we'd built mattered.

We weren't just building software. We were changing how businesses approached digital marketing. We were giving brands the power to understand audiences in a way they never had before. We were giving agencies the efficiency and data they needed to execute campaigns at scale.

And we weren't just competing—we were winning.

But with every win came new challenges. Growth meant we not only had to get more customers—we also had to be able to support them, to scale without breaking, to expand without losing what made us great. And I knew that if we wanted to take Tagger to the next level, we couldn't keep thinking like a startup.

We had to think bigger.

That meant looking beyond just growing our client base in the US —we had to think globally.

The Road to Global Expansion

Tagger was taking off, and the vision I had carried for years—the one that had consumed me—was finally becoming real. But I knew I couldn't take Tagger global on my own.

That's where Dave Dickman came in.

Dave had decades of experience in high-powered corporate roles, building and expanding divisions for Apple, Disney, Warner Bros, and Yahoo. He had lived and worked in India, London, and Hong Kong, navigating international markets with ease. At Apple, he had set up dozens of offices across the globe, built sales teams from the ground up, and launched products in some of the most competitive markets in the world.

He knew how to take a company from national to global—and that's exactly what Tagger needed.

I knew Dave personally—he grew up in Batesville, Indiana, the same small town my family was from. Of all the people I could go into business with, what were the odds it would be someone with roots in the same 7,000-person town? That felt like the universe tapping me on the shoulder.

At the time, Dave was President of Reelio, an influencer marketing platform that connected brands with creators—primarily on YouTube —to facilitate branded content collaborations.

Reelio's primary business, however, wasn't SaaS* (Software as a Service)—it was managed services. This meant they didn't just provide a platform—they ran influencer marketing campaigns for brands. Their tech wasn't nearly as robust as Tagger's, and even though they had a platform, their team actually used Tagger to run their campaigns.

---

* Software as a Service (SaaS) is a cloud-based software model where users access applications over the internet rather than installing them on local computers. SaaS companies typically operate on a subscription basis, providing ongoing updates, maintenance, and support.

We both had offices at WeWork in Santa Monica, and Dave and I crossed paths often. Whether it was grabbing coffee, catching up between meetings, or exchanging insights about the industry, I genuinely enjoyed hanging out with him. Over time, I found myself stopping by his office regularly, and every time I did, I could see how much his employees liked and respected him. He was a culture builder —the kind of leader who fostered loyalty and camaraderie. That resonated with me because that's exactly the kind of culture we had built at Tagger.

One day, I ran into him in the lobby of a brand we were both pitching to. As I walked in, he was walking out, grinning like he had just closed the deal. With his usual dry wit, he smirked and said, "Good luck."

Dave was an incredible salesman—effortlessly likable, sharp, and funny. I knew he had won them over the moment he shook their hands. His charm was undeniable, and judging by that smirk, he knew it too. It wasn't just confidence—it was the look of someone who had read the room, nailed his pitch, and left them smiling. And he knew exactly what was going to happen next.

I sat down and opened with "Reelio is our customer. They use our platform to run their campaigns."

I wouldn't have said that about any other client, but with Dave, it was a well-timed jab—one he saw coming before I even opened my mouth. It was a playful shot across the bow, a mix of respect and competition. And I took great pleasure calling him later that week to let him know we signed that deal.

But beyond the friendly rivalry, something was becoming increasingly clear—Dave wasn't being used to his full potential. He had built and expanded companies across the globe, yet here he was, pitching to brands in the US for a platform that wasn't even Reelio's primary business. It felt like a waste of his expertise.

We were growing fast, but my vision had always been bigger than just building a successful company—I wanted to take Tagger global. And I knew that if we were going to scale internationally, Dave was the guy to do it.

But convincing him wasn't easy.

He saw that Reelio was on the verge of an exit, and walking away before the payday wasn't the obvious choice. He had already put in the work, and the safe bet was to ride it out. Why leave stability for the uncertainty of another startup?

I had to show him that Tagger wasn't just another company—it was an opportunity to build something global, something far beyond just a modest exit. I wasn't asking him to take a leap just for the thrill of it—I was asking him to help build a global powerhouse.

Finally, he agreed—but he had one condition.

He wanted to be CEO.

I didn't care about titles. I cared about equity. I cared about the big win. I knew what Dave could bring to the table, and I knew that if we played this right, the valuation of the company would skyrocket.

So we split the responsibilities:

- Dave ran international expansion and marketing.
- I ran US sales and product development.
- Together, we managed finance and customer success.

And it worked.

By 2017, our international expansion was underway, starting with an office in London and a reseller in Canada.* From there, our global footprint took off—spanning Singapore, Australia, Brazil, France, Germany, and Africa.

We weren't just running a company anymore. We were building a global machine.

Expanding the Empire

By this point, it felt like I was living out of a suitcase.

Every month, I flew to New York for a week. Every other month, I was in Kraków, sitting with our development team, mapping out the next evolution of our platform. In between, it was LA, London,

---

* A reseller is a third-party partner who sells your product or service in a specific market, often handling sales and local support without requiring you to build a full in-house team.

Chicago—wherever the next big opportunity called. My life had become a relentless loop of airports, hotel rooms, and conference rooms, a blur of time zones and taxi rides, of red-eye flights and boardroom pitches.

I was always moving, always chasing, always pushing.

And it didn't dawn on me just how much I was traveling until one day, a package arrived at my house from Delta Airlines.

Inside was a sleek Tumi carry-on suitcase. Tucked inside was a card: "Congratulations on reaching One Million Miler™ status and being part of our most elite group of flyers."

I stared at it for a long time.

A million miles.

I had flown a million miles.

At first, I felt a surge of pride. That suitcase was a trophy—a testament to my grind, to the miles I had put between myself and failure. It meant I was making moves. That the sacrifice was paying off. That I was inching toward the dream I had carried with me since the beginning.

But then, standing in my own house with a suitcase that symbolized how rarely I was actually there, a different feeling crept in.

I had been gone *a lot.*

How many flights had I taken while my kids were at home? How many nights had I fallen asleep in some random hotel room while Brooks slept alone? How many school performances had I missed? How many moments had I traded for meetings and deals and strategy sessions?

And Sundays on the road? Those were the worst.

Sunday was the one day when I wasn't in meetings. No strategy sessions, no deals to chase, no client dinners. Just me, alone in some random city, walking the streets with nowhere to be. I had no reason to be in that city on a Sunday, no justification for sitting in a hotel room instead of being home with my family. No distractions. Just absence— an emptiness that no deal, no milestone, no first-class upgrade could ever fill.

Back home, the kids were at the rec center playing basketball. The family was having Sunday dinner. The small rituals of home were playing out without me, and I felt the full weight of it. I started calling it

"The Sunday Sads" because that's exactly what it was—the weight of everything I was missing hitting me hard.

In the noise of the week, I could push it aside. Convince myself it was worth it. But on Sundays, there was nowhere to hide from the truth.

And yet, I kept going.

I shook it off.

This was the price of building something big.

And I was willing to pay it.

Because I wasn't just clocking miles—I was on a mission.

The São Paulo Lesson

The grind never stopped. As soon as Dave opened a new office internationally, I'd fly there for two weeks to train the sales team and meet with prospective clients. Every country had its own intricacies, its own business culture, and I was learning all of it in real time.

When we launched our São Paulo, Brazil, office in February 2019, I flew down to train the team and land our first big deals. By the time I arrived, our team had already lined up meetings with twenty brands— our standard playbook for breaking into a new market. My job was to hit the ground running, pitching Tagger twenty to thirty times over the course of ten days, turning every meeting into real-time training for our new team.

On the way to our first meeting, I glanced at my watch and felt my stomach drop. We were going to be twenty minutes late—not just to any meeting, but to Ambev, the Brazilian subsidiary of AB InBev, the largest brewing company in the world. If there was one way to make a bad first impression, this was it.

Sitting in the thick of São Paulo's infamous traffic, I looked over at Carolina Pascowitch, our brilliant and talented Head of Brazil, who was behind the wheel. She looked completely unbothered, as if we were taking a leisurely Sunday drive through the countryside.

I, on the other hand, was silently spiraling.

At Tagger, being on time wasn't just a courtesy—it was a rule. We arrived at least twenty minutes early for every meeting to ensure laptops connected, demo loaded, and everything ran smoothly. I had been to too many pitches where the company's AV setup wasn't plug-and-play, forcing some poor IT guy to scramble at the last minute while we all stood there awkwardly.

So as we inched along through the gridlocked streets, I turned to Carolina, my frustration bubbling over.

"Carolina, we're going to be twenty minutes late. This is not good. I don't like being late to meetings. Can you at least call them and let them know?"

She smiled, completely at ease, and said, "Twenty minutes isn't late in Brazil. *I'm sure we'll be waiting for them.*"

I stared at her, dumbfounded.

Was she serious? Showing up half an hour late to a major meeting wasn't considered late? In my world, that was career suicide. But Carolina wasn't just calm—she was confident.

When we finally arrived at Ambev's office, I braced myself for the consequences. We checked in at the front desk, where the receptionist casually said, "You can head to the conference room. I'll let the team know you're here."

I sat down, still uneasy. And then . . . nothing happened. Ten minutes passed. Then fifteen. At the twenty-minute mark, the Ambev team strolled in, relaxed and smiling, as if we had just arrived.

Carolina shot me a knowing look. *You have a lot to learn about the Brazilian market.*

Brazilian Business Culture

São Paulo had more lessons in store for me than just being "on time" by being late.

In the US, business meetings followed a formula—walk in, shake hands, exchange a few pleasantries, and get straight to the point. Efficiency was king. In Brazil? Business was personal.

Instead of a handshake, men greeted women with a hug and a kiss on the cheek. Meetings didn't start with bullet points and slides—they started with stories. What you did last night, where you were going tonight, your favorite restaurants, your family, your weekend plans.

I remember sitting there, sipping my coffee, waiting for the pivot. The moment someone would steer the conversation toward the reason we were all in the room. But it didn't come. Five minutes passed. Ten. I wondered, Are we ever going to talk about work?

But that *was* the work.

Business in Brazil wasn't about closing deals—it was about building relationships. The connection came first. The contract came much later. It was the opposite of everything I had been conditioned to believe in the fast-paced, transactional world of US business.

I left Brazil, as I did every country, with a greater appreciation for the nuances of human connection and how culture shapes the way business is done. More than just a new market, it was a new way of thinking —one that prioritized trust and relationships over speed and efficiency.

And I carried that lesson with me.

Every country I traveled to had its own rhythm, its own unspoken rules about how deals were made and relationships were built. I learned to pay attention, to adapt, to integrate these insights into my own approach. I wasn't just selling a product anymore—I was learning how to connect with people in a way that transcended business.

Because at the end of the day, deals aren't made between companies. They're made between people. And the stronger the relationship, the easier everything else falls into place.

The Relentless Grind

This was my life.

Every month, another city. Another office to launch. Another sales team to train. Another market to learn.

In the span of a few weeks, I could be in New York for meetings, then off to Kraków working with our development team, then to Paris for a meeting with a luxury brand, then back to LA to catch up with the team before doing it all over again. I lived in airports, hotel lobbies, and boardrooms. My suitcase was never fully unpacked, my body never fully adjusted to a single time zone. I existed in a constant state of motion.

And I loved it.

At least, that's what I told myself.

Because there was something addictive about it. The pace. The urgency. The feeling that every flight, every meeting, every deal was pushing me closer to the vision I had been chasing for years.

I didn't just tolerate the grind—I embraced it. I told myself that this was what it took. That all the time away from home, all the sleepless nights, all the back-to-back meetings weren't just necessary—they were proof I was doing something meaningful.

But the thing about running at full speed is that you never stop to question where you're going.

I was so caught up in the momentum that I didn't allow myself to slow down long enough to ask, "At what cost?"

I told myself it was worth it. That this was temporary. That once we hit the next milestone, once we reached the next level, *then* I could breathe.

But the milestones kept moving.

And instead of slowing down, I doubled down.

Because to stop, even for a second, felt like failure.

Hustle at All Costs

There's an idea in business that you have to outwork everyone else to succeed. That if you're preparing for a meeting, your competitor is preparing harder. If you're pushing, they're pushing more. If you're sacrificing, they're sacrificing everything.

And I believed it completely.

It wasn't just a strategy—it was a survival instinct. If I wasn't obsessing over Tagger, someone else was, and that meant they could take what I was building.

So I worked. Harder. Longer. Faster.

I tried to out-hustle everyone around me, convinced it was the only way. The only way to be successful. The only way to prove . . . what exactly? That I was worthy? That I was smart enough? That I was the kind of guy who could build something big?

I didn't have time to think about those questions. There was no time. Because there was always another meeting. Another pitch. Another feature to build.

So I worked relentlessly. If an employee was underperforming, I'd step in and do their job for them until they either figured it out or I replaced them. There was a running joke at Tagger:

If Pete comes in to do your job, you're not going to be around for long.

At the time, I wore that like a badge of honor—proof that I was a great leader. But in reality, it was an early glimpse of how much of a control freak I had become. Instead of training my department heads and employees to meet my standards, I was micromanaging everything. If someone didn't meet my expectations, I'd take over.

I had no patience for inefficiency.

No tolerance for mistakes.

And in my mind, I wasn't just stepping in to fix problems—I was protecting something sacred. If you weren't doing your job, I convinced myself that I had to take over. Because you weren't just slowing down the business—you were getting in my way. My way to fulfilling my life's dream.

Because this wasn't just a company to me. It wasn't just a vehicle for financial success. It was proof.

Proof that I mattered.

Proof that I was as great as my grandfather.

I was chasing more than a financial milestone—I was chasing validation. Chasing the feeling that if I could build something big enough, sell it for enough, make enough people see my success, then maybe, just maybe, I would finally feel like I *was* enough.

I had spent a lifetime building an identity around this belief. The belief that success equaled worth, that achievement equaled love. So when an employee wasn't doing their job, it wasn't just an operational inefficiency or a bump in the road. They weren't just threatening the company. They were threatening my identity.

Because if things started slipping through the cracks, if mistakes piled up, if we lost momentum, and the company wasn't thriving, what did that say about me? Did that mean my grandfather would have done it better?

I wasn't just micromanaging to keep the business running—I was micromanaging to keep my identity intact.

And in my mind, that meant there was no room for weakness. No room for inefficiency. No room for anything less than perfection.

So I gripped tighter.

I didn't delegate—I took over.

I didn't trust—I controlled.

And I justified it all with the belief that I had to. That if I didn't step in, if I didn't push harder, then everything I had built would fall apart.

The problem was, the tighter I held on, the more exhausted I became. And the more exhausted I became, the more the cracks started to show. I would get frustrated with employees for not meeting my expectations, even though the truth was, I hadn't set them up for success. I had built a company that revolved around me—my standards, my pace, my obsessive need to control. And that wasn't leadership.

That was fear disguised as productivity.

The Identity Paradox

We spend our lives constructing identities—shaped by our upbringing, our environment, our achievements, and the expectations we place on ourselves—only to realize later that this very construction is what limits us. We mistake who we are for who we've been conditioned to be, and because we're attached to that version of ourselves, we defend it, protect it, and reinforce it—often at the cost of our own growth.

Our identities feel like absolute truths, but they're just stories we've told ourselves long enough to believe. *I'm a CEO. I'm a leader. I'm a builder. I'm the responsible one. I take care of everyone. I don't do spiritual stuff. That's not me. I'm not creative. I'm not an artist. I'm not the kind of person who takes risks.*

We don't realize that these statements aren't truths. These identities are simply limitations we impose on ourselves.

The greatest illusion of identity is that it's fixed—that once we *become* something, we must remain it. We tell ourselves that stepping outside of it would be betrayal, that if we let go of the person we worked so hard to become, we'll lose everything. But in reality, identity is meant to evolve. Holding too tightly to a certain persona—whether it's *the entrepreneur, the high achiever, the provider,* or *the strong one*—keeps us from discovering what's waiting on the other side.

We get lost in the identity of who we *think* we are rather than who we *truly* are. We become so entangled in the role we've crafted—whether it's *the leader, the fixer, the responsible one*—that we stop questioning if it still serves us. The more successful we become in an identity, the harder it is to step away from it. It feels like undoing everything we've built, like walking away from certainty into the unknown.

We don't just adopt these identities—we reinforce them, often without realizing it. They run on autopilot, shaping our decisions, our reactions, and our beliefs about what's possible. And their primary goal? Survival. The moment we start questioning them—*Maybe I shouldn't do this* or *Maybe this isn't serving me*—they fight back. That inner voice gets louder: *You can't change who you are. This is too hard. Let's start tomorrow.*

It's not just resistance—it's self-preservation. Because to the identity we've built, change feels like death.

But that's the paradox: True freedom isn't found in reinforcing who we are—it's found in allowing ourselves to become something more. The identities we cling to are often outdated survival mechanisms, built in response to wounds we don't even remember acquiring. *The overachiever* might have been a child who only felt seen when they excelled. *The provider* might have grown up in a home where love was earned through sacrifice. *The strong one* may have learned early on that vulnerability was a weakness, so they buried it to be respected.

And yes, we had to become those identities to survive—but survival isn't the same as fulfillment. When we mistake the identity we built for who we truly are, we stop growing. We stop listening to the deeper pull inside us, the one that whispers that there's something more.

The question isn't whether we should abandon our identities but rather, What would happen if we loosened our grip? What if we let ourselves explore beyond the version of us we've spent so long reinforcing? What if instead of fearing the unknown, we stepped into it with curiosity?

Because at the end of the day, identity isn't a fixed destination. It's a doorway. And on the other side of it? That's where our true journey begins.

Integration, Not Elimination

As I learned while working with Concetta, the goal isn't to destroy these identities—it's to integrate them. To recognize them without being ruled by them. To hold them lightly rather than gripping them for dear life. To acknowledge and love them rather than wage war against them. Because when we stop resisting who we are, we create space for who we might become. And in that openness, something incredible happens— we become receptive. Receptive to reinvention, to discovering parts of ourselves we never knew existed, to the idea that purpose isn't something we find—it's something that reveals itself when we stop clinging to the version of ourselves we think we need to be. And when you fully surrender to that, your true purpose unfolds in the most unexpected and magical way.

Fueling the Machine

By 2021, Tagger was firing on all cylinders. We had built an internationally recognized platform, expanded into multiple countries, and had some of the biggest brands and agencies in the world as clients. We were no longer a scrappy startup trying to prove ourselves—we had real market dominance.

But growth comes with a cost. Scaling a company isn't just about winning deals—it's about sustaining them. The bigger we got, the more complex the business became. We needed to hire more engineers to support our ever-growing product, more salespeople to chase bigger deals, more customer success to retain our clients. Running Tagger wasn't just about innovation anymore—it was about operational excellence. And that required serious capital.

That's when Five Elms Capital entered the picture. Based in Kansas City, Five Elms is a private equity firm specializing in fast-growing software companies. They knew the SaaS space, they understood our vision, and most importantly, they had the resources to take us to the next level.

Raising money is never just about the check—it's about who you're getting into business with. Five Elms had a reputation for being smart, strategic, and relentless in their pursuit of scaling businesses. But they also had one core belief that struck me from the very first meeting:

"We don't lose."

They weren't just betting on Tagger. They were betting on an exit.

When Five Elms Capital invested $23 million into Tagger for a minority stake, it was a sign that we weren't just a successful startup anymore—we were a company on the path to a major acquisition. The stakes were higher than ever.

And when they invested, they told me something that stuck in my head:

"When you think it's time to sell, it's time to sell."

At the time, I didn't fully appreciate what that meant. I was still deep in the grind, running on the hamster wheel, obsessed with pushing the company to the next level. But looking back, I see it now.

I wasn't just driving growth—I was living in fear of losing everything.

I had invested everything into this company—my money, my time, my energy, my family. Tagger wasn't just a business—it was my identity, my future, the thing that would finally make everything worth it. And as the company got bigger, as the stakes got higher, and as the reality of a successful exit got closer, my drive to succeed wasn't fueled by passion anymore—it was fueled by fear. Fear of losing everything. Fear of being a failure.

I had spent years grinding, sacrificing, pushing myself to the brink, convinced that this was the path to freedom. But instead of feeling closer to peace, I felt more trapped than ever. The pressure was suffocating. Every day, I was consumed with the thought that one wrong move, one misstep, one competitor outpacing us, and it could all slip through my fingers.

It wasn't just about my own success anymore—it was about my family's future, my employees' livelihoods, my investors' expectations. I carried it all. And the more I held on, the heavier it became.

I thought I was in control. I believed that if I just worked harder, if I just pushed through, I could force the outcome I wanted. But looking back, I see it clearly now—fear had taken the wheel.

And when fear is running the show, you don't make decisions from a place of trust or vision—you make them from a place of survival. My eye wasn't just on building the company anymore. It was on securing an exit before everything collapsed.

I convinced myself that once I sold, the pressure would be gone. That the fear would disappear. That I could finally breathe. That I would be free. And finally—finally—I would be happy.

The finish line wasn't some distant dream. It was right around the corner.

First trip to New York City—pitching to anyone who would listen. Walking the streets with Dick Hillenbrand (left), chasing the dream. December 2015.

Introducing Tagger in Brazil—our first step into Latin America. February 2019.

Speaking at the Collision Conference in Toronto, Canada. June 2022.

Our Tagger off-site at Alisal Ranch in Solvang, California. Always a blast with this team. October 2022.

11

THE SALE

"It always seems impossible until it's done."
—Nelson Mandela

In December 2022, I received an email from Jason Rechel, Vice President of Investor Relations and Corporate Development at Sprout Social, Inc. Sprout Social is a social media management platform that helps brands schedule posts, engage with audiences, and analyze performance on social media. If you're a brand using social media to promote your products—and let's be honest, they all do—you need a platform to manage your social profiles, content, and audience interactions all in one place. That's what Sprout Social's software enabled brands to do. And compared to Tagger, they were massive.

With over 1,000 employees, $250M+ in revenue, and 30,000 customers, Sprout was a leader in the social media analytics space. They were publicly traded on the NASDAQ and had built an incredible reputation. But there was one glaring gap in their offering: influencer marketing.

Throughout the years of building Tagger, I often told potential investors that Sprout Social would be the perfect acquirer for us. Their customers already relied on influencer marketing as a key part of their social media strategy, and adding Tagger to their already powerful platform felt like a no-brainer. So when I received Jason's email, I had to play it cool—but inside, I was buzzing.

Jason informed me that their CEO and co-founder, Justyn Howard, lived in Los Angeles and wanted to meet. Hiding my excitement, I casually replied, "Nice to meet you, Jason. Would be happy to meet Justyn." We exchanged a few emails leading up to Christmas, but then—radio silence.

The Waiting Game

Shit.

Did the perfect acquirer for Tagger just disappear?

Sprout's customers were already leveraging influencer marketing as a key part of their strategy—but they were managing those campaigns on other platforms, including Tagger. I was convinced Tagger was the solution they needed. Sure, by 2022, the influencer space was crowded—throw a rock, and you'd hit a competitor. But no one had built what we had.

Our competitors all had their own angles, but most avoided one of the toughest markets—advertising agencies. Agencies were notoriously demanding—they needed robust reporting, seamless integrations, and a level of flexibility that most competitors simply couldn't (or wouldn't) provide. The common belief was that agencies were more trouble than they were worth.

We saw it differently.

Tagger thrived with agencies because our foundation was built on them. Our first ten clients were agencies, and instead of shying away, we leaned in. We built our platform to handle the complexity, the high expectations, the rapid changes. That approach paid off—we secured deals with nearly every major global advertising holding company, proving that if we could build something powerful enough for the toughest clients in the world, it would be powerful enough for everyone.

We didn't just serve the biggest brands and agencies—we worked alongside them, adapting to their evolving needs and setting the industry standard.

Tagger was the solution Sprout needed.

Still, months passed—and no word from Jason.

Meanwhile, we were growing fast. My calendar was packed—almost every hour filled with customer calls and meetings with potential partners. My Chief of Staff, the brilliant and unshakable Leise Trueblood, kept everything running like clockwork. Eight-hour days of back-to-back Zoom calls. I barely had time to eat lunch.

An email from Sprout would've been a welcome sign they were serious—but I wasn't holding my breath. After months of silence, Sprout Social was the last thing on my mind.

Paradox of Attachment

For nearly a decade, I had been on an emotional roller coaster—buyers showing interest, then ghosting. Venture capitalists courting us, then disappearing. Highs, lows, almosts, and maybes. I told myself I had learned not to get too excited until the money was in the bank. That I was detached. That I could handle rejection. But the truth? I was still deeply attached.

Attached to the outcome.

Attached to the validation.

Attached to the idea that this deal would be the moment everything finally clicked into place.

In business—and in life—attachment is suffering. The more we grip on to something—whether it's a deal, a goal, or an idea of how things *should* play out—the more we set ourselves up for frustration, anxiety, and disappointment. And paradoxically, the more attached we are, the more we actually repel the very thing we want.

That's the trap of attachment. It tricks you into believing that your happiness, your worth, your peace all hinge on something external. That once you get the deal, the title, the number in your bank account, then —finally—you'll feel whole. But that's the greatest lie in modern society.

We are conditioned from birth to believe that fulfillment comes from something *out there.* If you drink this, you'll be happy. If you buy this, you'll look beautiful. If you take this pill, you'll feel better. Since we were kids, we've been fed the idea that something external will complete us—through TV commercials, billboards, magazine covers, and now, social media. And we believed it.

But the truth? There is no silver bullet. No single purchase, achievement, or milestone will make us whole. Because when we tie our happiness to something external, we don't just chase it—we become *dependent* on it. And once we depend on it, we live in fear of losing it. What once made us happy now becomes a source of anxiety. The validation we sought turns into the insecurity of "What if I can't keep this up?" The success we craved becomes the pressure of "What if this all disappears?"

That's why one of my favorite Buddhist mantras—something I repeat to myself and remind my kids of all the time—is *the only thing permanent in life is impermanence.*

Everything in life—our experiences, relationships, emotions, even our physical selves—is in a constant state of flux. Nothing stays the same forever. And the more we embrace that, the less we suffer. The less we cling. The less we resist change. Because real peace isn't found in holding on—it's found in learning to let go. And ironically, the moment I started loosening my grip, things started falling into place. The second I stopped obsessing over whether or not Sprout would come back, the universe delivered the answer I had been waiting for.

On a random Monday in early March, Jason emailed me again.

At first, I was slightly annoyed. I hadn't heard from them in over three months, and I hated wasting time on fishing expeditions. But this email was different.

"The executive team will be in Los Angeles and wants to meet with the Tagger team."

This wasn't just an exploratory conversation. This was a face-to-face meeting. This was serious.

I kept my reply short and neutral: "Sounds good. We'll be here."

But inside? I was pumped.

The Meeting

When the Sprout team walked through our doors, I knew this was real.

In the room were three key players, each with a distinct role in determining the fate of the deal. Jason Rechel, the deal guy, was focused on ROI—making sure the numbers made sense and that the acquisition would drive real value. Justyn Howard, the CEO and co-founder, was the product guy. He had built Sprout into a powerhouse and knew great technology when he saw it. His dilemma was clear—should Sprout build its own influencer marketing solution or buy the best one on the market? Then there was Ryan Barretto, Sprout's President and future CEO—the revenue guy. A sharp operator with a background at Salesforce, he was responsible for ensuring that any acquisition would fuel scalable, profitable growth.

The stakes were high—higher than they had ever been. This wasn't just another pitch or another round of negotiations. This was the moment that could change everything. The deal had to be right, not just for us but for Sprout's executive team, their shareholders, and their long-term vision. The product had to impress—not just functionally but in a way that made acquiring us the obvious, undeniable choice over building their own solution. And most importantly, we had to show them who we were—not just what we built but *why* we built it. They needed to feel the conviction behind every decision, every line of code, every late night we had poured into Tagger.

But conviction alone wasn't enough. Deals like this weren't made in product demos or term sheets—they were made in conversations. In connection. In trust.

I loved the beginnings of meetings. Before the numbers, the negotiations, and the high-stakes discussions, there was the simple act of getting to know people. Over the years, I had come to understand that business wasn't just about deals—it was about relationships. And relationships were built through curiosity. I had learned to ask better questions—the kind that revealed who someone really was. What they cared about. What drove them. What made them tick.

It made things even easier when the people sitting across from me were the kind of guys you'd actually want to grab a beer with. Justyn,

Jason, and Ryan were solid Midwestern guys—likable, down-to-earth, and easy to talk to. They carried themselves with a quiet confidence, the kind that didn't need to prove anything. There was an immediate sense of familiarity, like I wasn't just sitting down with executives from a publicly traded company but with people I could actually see myself working alongside.

There was a natural ease to the conversation, the kind that makes you feel like you're not just pitching a deal but opening a door to something bigger. I could tell they weren't the type to be impressed by fluff. They wanted substance. They wanted something real. And we were ready to give it to them.

After introductions, I synced my laptop to the big TV on the wall and jumped straight into the demo—something I had done over 8,000 times in the last eight and a half years. No PowerPoint slides. No sandbox demo.* Just the live platform, in real time. Whether we were pitching to a potential customer, investor, or acquirer, we always led with the actual product. No smoke and mirrors—because we didn't need them. Tagger's product spoke for itself.

Justyn was visibly impressed. As I navigated through the platform, showcasing its capabilities in real time, his eyes were locked on the screen. He nodded as I walked through the workflow, making small comments about the speed and seamlessness of the interface. "This is really fast," he remarked, almost to himself. That was all the validation I needed.

The speed wasn't an accident. It was one of the many core parts of what made Tagger different. Credit for that went to our CTO, Bartek Radziszewski—a database wizard who had spent years optimizing every query, every process, every line of code to ensure the platform wasn't just functional but lightning-fast and rock-solid reliable. Tagger processed and analyzed billions of data points in real time, ensuring that any query delivered instant results—no small feat. Achieving this level of speed and efficiency required an immense amount of engineering precision, optimization, and infrastructure scaling. Unlike our competi-

---

* A sandbox demo is a controlled testing environment—a polished, preloaded version of the software designed to avoid hiccups.

tors, where users were often met with frustrating loading screens and delays, Tagger provided a seamless, frictionless experience. Every click, every search, every report was designed to be immediate and intuitive, because in high-stakes marketing, speed isn't just a convenience—it's a competitive advantage. Agencies and brands ran high-volume campaigns with millions of data points, and any lag, any delay, would slow them down. That was unacceptable. Tagger didn't just meet expectations—it set the standard.

After the demo, we dove into the business side—Tagger's history, our cap table, revenue growth, customer base, and all the key SaaS metrics that acquirers care about. It was a numbers game now. Were we profitable? What was our churn rate? How sticky was the platform? Could this be scaled across Sprout's 30,000 customers?

Fortunately, we had all the right answers because Dennis Lin, Tagger's Head of Finance, had prepared us for every possible question, every scenario, every financial angle they might challenge. He was the most capable finance person I had ever worked with. While most finance professionals fixate on problems, Dennis focused on solutions. He wasn't afraid to make assumptions in a financial model, and nine times out of ten, he was spot on. Without him, Tagger wouldn't have become the success it did.

They asked smart, strategic questions, testing to see if there were any weak points in our story. Jason flipped through his notes, asking about ARR growth. Ryan drilled into expansion revenue and customer retention. Justyn was more interested in the product roadmap—where we were headed next. Their poker faces were good, but I had been in enough meetings like this to recognize the signs.

I could see it in the way Justyn kept circling back to certain features, in the way Ryan asked about layering Tagger into Sprout's sales pipeline, in how Jason was already thinking through deal structures. The chemistry in the room had shifted. This wasn't just a demo anymore—it was a conversation about the future.

The Closing Pitch

At the end of the meeting, I decided to be blunt. There was no point in dancing around the obvious—we had the best platform, the right customer base, the right cap table, and they knew it.

I leaned forward and laid it out. "You have the ability to scale our technology across your 30,000 customers quickly. I know Tagger will drive incredible value for you and your customers. If you don't buy us, that's totally fine. But do me a favor—don't buy one of our shitty competitors. You'll make a splash in the market, disrupt the industry for a month, and then your customers will realize the platform sucks, and they'll all leave."

The room went quiet for half a second before a few chuckles broke the silence from their side of the table. It was direct. A little cocky. But 100% true.

And I wanted them to hear it.

The reality was, if they wanted to add influencer marketing to their offering, they had three choices: spend two years building a platform they didn't have time for, acquire the best and integrate it seamlessly, or settle for a lesser option and waste valuable time realizing their mistake. The data, the tech, the customer relationships—all of it pointed in one direction. They had an opportunity to dominate this space overnight by acquiring Tagger. Any other path would be a gamble.

We shook hands, exchanged pleasantries, and wrapped up the meeting. As they walked out the door, I knew we had made an impression.

Two weeks later, we had a term sheet.

The Term Sheet

After nine years of grinding, pushing, and sacrificing, the term sheet landed in my inbox like a long-awaited finish line appearing on the horizon—close enough to taste, but still requiring one final sprint. The expected close date—August 3. The price—not quite where we wanted it, but close enough to get serious.

Dave and I wasted no time calling up our investment bankers, Jon Guido and Doug Hurst from AGC Partners, to share the news. We had met Jon and Doug just two years after launching Tagger, back when we were a scrappy software company with big dreams and not a lot of traction. Most investment bankers wouldn't give us the time of day back then. The usual response? "Call me when you get big."

But not Jon and Doug.

While others dismissed us, they invested in us—answering our calls, offering market insights, and advising us on funding rounds even when there was no immediate payday for them. And when we didn't call, they called us. They believed in the industry and, more importantly, they believed in us.

I jumped right in. "Did you guys see the term sheet we sent over?"

Jon barely hesitated. "Yeah, we saw it. The price is too low, and August 3rd is aggressive. We'll call Jason and see what we can do. But guys, just so you know—whatever price we land on, Sprout is going to try and crush that number in due diligence. It's not a reflection of your company. It's just how deals are done."

I gave a half-grin. "Then you'd better get us a high price." It was a joke—but not really.

The next day, Jon and Doug called back with a new number—$140 million. All cash.

If I had heard that number back in 2015, I would have fallen off my chair. Back then, Tagger was just an idea, a scrappy startup with no customers, no revenue, and no guarantee it would ever turn into anything meaningful. The thought of someone offering nine figures for something I had built would have felt like pure fantasy.

But by 2023, things were different. Tagger wasn't just an idea anymore—it was a thriving company with a global presence, an industry-leading product, and a roster of blue-chip clients. We had spent nearly a decade proving our worth, winning over agencies, brands, and investors, and scaling our platform to handle billions of data points in real time. We had battled competitors, navigated a global pandemic, and fought tooth and nail for every inch of market share.

So when the offer came in at $140 million, it didn't feel like a lucky break—it felt earned. It wasn't just a validation of what we had built—it was a reflection of the blood, sweat, and resilience that had gone into every single decision along the way. It was the right number, at the right time.

Drowning in Due Diligence

A week later, due diligence began.

If I had known what was coming, I would have booked a weeklong vacation just to mentally prepare. Maybe two.

Sprout Social was a public company, which meant this wasn't going to be your typical look-at-the-financials-and-sign-the-paperwork kind of due diligence process. I expected it to be thorough—after all, they had shareholders to answer to, compliance regulations to follow, and risk factors to mitigate.

But *thorough* didn't even come close.

On Day One, we received an Excel spreadsheet with over 300 line items—requests for financials, legal documents, technical specs, and customer data.

They wanted to see, hear, and touch every single detail of our business. Every document. Every line of code. Every financial transaction.

Nothing was off-limits.

And just as we were wrapping our heads around that first wave of requests, another spreadsheet arrived.

Another 300 lines.

And this continued for weeks.

It wasn't just a time-consuming process—it was all-consuming. Nearly all 120 employees were pulled into the process at some point. Engineers were asked to pull reports on platform stability and security. The finance team had to reconcile every number, going back years. Sales had to provide detailed customer histories and contracts. Legal had to dig up paperwork we barely remembered signing.

The problem? While we were knee-deep in due diligence, we still had a business to run. New deals still had to close. Customers still needed support. Bugs still had to be fixed. Employees still had to be managed. And yet, day after day, we were pulled deeper into a legal and financial vortex that made it nearly impossible to focus on anything else.

I kept hearing Jon's words in the back of my mind—*Sprout is going to try and crush that number in due diligence.* Dave, Dennis, and I weren't about to give them any excuse to knock down our purchase price. If sales started dipping or customer retention wavered, they'd use it as leverage to renegotiate. Jon and Doug had seen it happen countless times—acquirers getting cold feet, suddenly questioning the value of a company because of a minor fluctuation in numbers or uncovering a backlog of technical improvements that hadn't been addressed. A dip in sales? A slight uptick in customer churn? Any of it could be used as leverage to chip away at the purchase price.

We weren't about to let that happen. We had worked too hard for this. So while we were drowning in legal requests, financial audits, and technical deep dives, Dave and I made sure we stayed focused on keeping Tagger strong. Every contract needed to be renewed. Every deal needed to close. Every customer needed to feel supported. If we started slipping, even a little, I feared Sprout would smell blood in the water. And after nearly a decade of building this company, I wasn't about to give them a reason to second-guess what they were buying.

I remember one night, long past midnight, sitting in my office, my eyes burning from staring at yet another round of due diligence requests. My inbox was a war zone—flooded with emails from lawyers, accountants, auditors, compliance officers, investment bankers, and Sprout's executive team. And that was on top of the 300 daily emails and Slack messages from our tech, sales, customer success, marketing, finance, and HR teams. Everyone needed something. And they all needed it yesterday.

I shot off an email to Dave: *If this deal doesn't close, I'm not sure we'll survive.*

And I meant it.

We were running on fumes. There weren't enough hours in the day to keep Tagger operating at full speed while juggling the relentless demands of due diligence. The lawyers, the auditors, the compliance teams, the shareholders—and most importantly, our customers—all needed our attention.

At this point, it wasn't just about closing the deal. It was about making it through without breaking.

The Deal That Wouldn't Die

Over the summer, the deal changed constantly. One minute, it was on. The next, it was off. Every time we thought we were in the clear, some tiny issue would suddenly snowball into a catastrophe, threatening to derail everything.

A seemingly minor legal clause? Now it's a multi-day debate. A small tweak in the purchase agreement? Now the lawyers need to "circle back" for the tenth time. A single word in a contract? Now there's another round of calls, emails, and redlines.

To Sprout's credit, the one thing that never changed was the price. They operated with integrity throughout the process, never attempting to lowball us or backtrack on their initial offer—a rarity in acquisitions of this scale. But at some point, the price almost felt inconsequential compared to the nonstop demands coming from every direction. Lawyers. Due diligence advisors. Investors. Sprout. Everyone had their own agenda. Everyone had nonnegotiables.

And the only people who seemed to be compromising? Dave and me.

It felt like we were being pulled in every direction, constantly bending to meet the needs of lawyers, investors, compliance teams, and Sprout's due diligence advisors. Every day, there was a new demand, a new nonnegotiable, a new fire to put out. And every time we thought we had cleared one hurdle, another one appeared. It was exhausting. The kind of exhaustion that seeps into your bones, the kind that makes you question why you ever started this in the first place.

If it weren't for the personal development work I was doing with Greg Lawrence at the time, I don't know how I would have handled it. Because whenever things seemed like they were falling apart—which was, by my estimate, every few hours—Dave would call me, livid.

"Dude, this could screw us over! Why aren't you pissed right now?"

He wasn't wrong. The stakes were enormous. A single misstep, a bad negotiation, or a last-minute clause slipping through the cracks could cost us millions. And yet, instead of reacting, I kept coming back to what Greg had drilled into me:

"They're just doing their problem."

It probably annoyed the hell out of Dave, but that phrase became my anchor. It was a reminder that none of this was personal. The lawyers weren't scheming to make our lives miserable—they were just doing what lawyers do, minimizing risk and protecting their clients. The investors weren't intentionally trying to squeeze us dry—they were just looking after their returns. Even Sprout, despite all their last-minute requests and relentless scrutiny, wasn't trying to play games—they were making sure they were getting what they paid for.

Everyone was just running their own programming. Their fears, their experiences, their professional obligations—all playing out in real-time.

Once I saw that, I could let go. I could step back and see the deal for what it really was. Not a battle to be won, not a war over leverage or control, but a negotiation between humans, each of whom had their own pressures, their own insecurities, their own motivations.

And that changed everything.

I stopped reacting. I stopped taking every demand as an attack. I stopped feeling like I had to fight for every inch. Instead, I focused on navigating the process with as much clarity and patience as possible. Because the truth was, the deal would get done. The price was set. The terms were being finalized. The acquisition press release was approved. And the more I stayed present and level-headed, the better I could ensure that we walked away with what we wanted.

August 3, 2023

Despite four months of chaos, an unforgiving due diligence process, and more near-collapses than I could count, the deal finally closed.

On August 3, 2023, we officially sold Tagger to Sprout Social for $140,000,000—all cash.

The final signatures were in. The deal was done.

Dave and I looked at each other through our computer screens on Zoom—drained, exhilarated, and barely able to process the moment. Exhausted but victorious. The weight of nearly a decade of work, of sleepless nights, of all the times we thought it might never happen, finally lifted.

That nine-digit exit I had dreamed about since I was young? It was real.

I leaned back in my chair, exhaled, and tried to let it sink in.

Nine years. Thousands of pitches. Countless sacrifices. Millions of miles on planes. Waking up in hotel rooms and forgetting which city I was in. Rushing from meetings to airports, from airports to meetings, living in a blur of conference rooms, investor decks, and late-night emails. Every ounce of energy, every drop of focus, every waking thought had been poured into building this company, growing it, selling it. And now, with a few final signatures, it was over.

This was the moment I had spent my entire life working toward. The validation. The security. The proof that I had built something real, something lasting. The nine-figure exit that, once upon a time, I believed would be the defining moment of my career—of my life.

So why did it feel like something was missing?

I closed my laptop, exhaled, and stepped outside. The night air was cool against my skin, the kind of crispness that usually makes you feel awake, alive. But instead of feeling weightless, instead of the expected flood of relief, something heavy settled in my chest.

This was supposed to be the finish line. The moment where everything clicked into place.

So why did it feel like I had just crossed one finish line, only to realize it was just another starting point?

12

BEYOND THE FINISH LINE

"We spend our lives searching for what we already are."
—Rumi

T he sale of Tagger should have been the ultimate victory. After nine years of grinding, pushing, sacrificing—I had finally made it. It was the kind of exit most entrepreneurs dream of. And I had done it.

It was everything I had worked for. The childhood dream of building a global business? Check. The validation of creating something valuable enough for a public company to buy? Check. Financial security for my family? Check.

And yet, sitting at our cottage in northern Michigan, looking out at the still water, I felt nothing.

Actually, that's not true. I felt something. But it wasn't the euphoria I expected. It wasn't the overwhelming sense of accomplishment or relief I had spent years fantasizing about. It was emptiness.

The months leading up to the sale had been brutal. I had spent the entire summer locked in my office, working fifteen hours a day to get the deal across the finish line. When people talk about startups, they think the hardest part is launching—getting that first customer, finding product-market fit. But let me tell you, the exit stage is an entirely different beast.

Deals like this don't happen cleanly. They shift, twist, and turn until you feel like you're losing your grip on reality. Ours changed at least a hundred times—each shift feeling like we were starting from scratch, each change threatening to bring the entire deal to the brink of collapse.

It wasn't just business. It was psychological warfare.

And the longer it dragged on, the more I was convinced of one thing: If I could just get this deal done, I'd finally be free.

But when the final signature came through, and the merger agreement was done, I didn't feel free. In fact, I felt miserable.

The Moment It Sank In

Most people would have popped champagne, thrown a party, gotten completely wasted. They would have booked a table at the nicest restaurant in town, ordered the most expensive bottle of wine, and toasted to their success until the early hours of the morning. They would have celebrated loud and large, reveling in the moment, soaking in the accomplishment.

But we didn't.

Brooks and I just sat on the couch that night, talking like we always did.

We talked about the sale for a bit—about how insane the last few months had been—but honestly, it already felt like old news. The moment had come and gone, and life was still just life.

You'd think we would have at least had a drink to celebrate, but we had quit drinking two years earlier—a decision that had fundamentally reshaped how we experienced moments like this. For most of our lives, alcohol had been the automatic punctuation for success, stress, joy, or anything in between. It was how we celebrated, how we unwound, how we processed the highs and lows. And for years, I had imagined this moment through that same lens—a packed bar with friends, rounds of shots, a toast with expensive champagne. That's just what you did when you hit a milestone like this.

But sobriety had stripped away the distractions, leaving me face-to-face with the raw truth of every experience. There was no numbing, no artificial high—just the reality of the moment, exactly as it was. And as I sat there, staring at the walls of our cottage, feeling more empty than victorious, I felt it:

Brooks knew. She always knew.

"You don't feel how you thought you would, do you?"

I sighed, rubbing my hands over my face. "Not even close."

She didn't rush to fill the silence. She just watched me, waiting.

"I guess I thought I'd feel different," I finally admitted.

"What do you mean by 'different'?"

"I don't know. I thought I'd feel relieved. Accomplished. Like everything had clicked into place. Instead, I just feel kind of . . . everything and nothing at the same time."

She nodded, her eyes warm with understanding. "So what were you expecting?"

I exhaled, staring down at the floor. "Like I'd finally arrived. Like I'd done it. Like the heavens would open up and a giant beam of light would shine down on me or something."

She laughed—at the image, at the absurdity of expecting divine validation for selling a company. Then she squeezed my hand, her voice steady and certain.

"You know, sometimes the only thing to do is sit with it. Just be with whatever comes up."

I knew she was right, but sitting with my emotions—actually feeling them, untangling them—had never come easily to me. Because the truth was, I wasn't feeling just one thing—I was feeling *everything*, all at once. Relief, sadness, freedom, disappointment. And something I didn't want to admit.

Embarrassment.

Because what kind of ungrateful asshole sells his company for $140 million and feels bad about it?

That familiar voice in my head was having a field day—*Oh, poor*

Pete. Just made millions. Cue the world's tiniest violin. Must be hard, huh?

I knew how ridiculous it sounded. How many people would kill to be in my position? And yet, the feelings were real. The conflict was real. And so was the frustration of not being able to untangle it all, to put a clean label on what I was experiencing.

But I told myself it was just exhaustion. That after months of late nights, endless meetings, and the pressure of closing the deal, I just needed sleep.

Tomorrow will be different, I thought.

Tomorrow, I'd wake up and finally feel the weight of my accomplishment.

Tomorrow, I'd finally feel worthy.

The Morning After

I woke up the next morning, stretched, and looked up.

No golden light streaming from the heavens. No divine revelation. No overwhelming rush of fulfillment.

Just me. Still me.

Life didn't stop to acknowledge my so-called arrival. It just kept moving—like it always did.

The coffee still needed brewing. The kids still needed to be woken up for their summer jobs. The emails were still piling up in my inbox.

Sure, people congratulated me—sent messages, said, "Great job," gave me a pat on the back. But the reality? No one really cared—not in the way I had secretly hoped. It didn't change how they saw me. It didn't make them like me more or less. To them, it was just another day.

Of course, my parents and family were proud. They knew how hard I had worked over the past nine years, how much I had sacrificed. But they didn't love me any more than they had the day before. Nothing had changed—except for the number in my bank account. And honestly, I didn't even care about that.

Was it the lack of acknowledgment? The realization that the world hadn't shifted just because I had sold my company?

I didn't want to call it depression—because that felt like admitting weakness—but I knew I wasn't myself. I was in a funk. That's what I'd call it. A funk. And funks don't last forever. I'd snap out of it soon, and the pride would kick in. I'd finally feel what I was supposed to—relief, accomplishment, peace.

But instead, sitting there in the silence, I felt more lost than ever.

Staring out at the glassy, endless stretch of Lake Michigan, the truth hit me like a ton of bricks: *There is no finish line.*

There is no moment when you cross over and suddenly become fulfilled. The entire game is rigged against that reality. And the second I realized it, my "funk" turned into complete depression. Because in that moment, I understood something that made me feel completely unmoored: *The chase never ends.*

The second you achieve one milestone, another appears in its place. You make your first million, and suddenly, you're chasing five. You close a big deal, and before you can celebrate, you're worried about the next one. You sell the company, and instead of the love, the validation, the happiness you expected—there's just *nothing*.

I had spent years sprinting toward this moment, convinced that once I got here, the race would be over. That I'd finally stop feeling like I had something to prove. That I'd finally silence the voices in my head telling me I wasn't enough. That I'd finally—*finally*—be happy.

But I wasn't.

Because the moment doesn't exist.

For my entire life, I had been operating under the illusion that some external event would fix what was broken inside of me. That success would erase the doubt. That money would fill the void. That finally proving myself—to the teachers who said I wouldn't make it, to the world that had underestimated me, to the people who had written me off before I even had a chance—would heal the part of me that still believed they were right.

But it didn't.

And that realization crushed me. Because if this *wasn't* the thing that would make me feel whole, then what would?

Happiness and fulfillment now seemed like a task *more impossible* than selling a company. I had just pulled off what so many only dream of, and it still wasn't enough.

And for the first time in my life, I didn't have an answer.

I had spent years believing that if I just worked hard enough, pushed long enough, and achieved big enough, I would *earn* my way to happiness. That fulfillment was something I could *win*. But now, standing at the peak of everything I had built, I realized I had been climbing the wrong mountain.

I had no plan for *this*. No strategy. No next move.

And in that space of uncertainty—where my usual instincts of force and control had always served me—they were finally failing, and I felt something I wasn't used to feeling.

Depressed.

Rod and the Breaking Point

But the universe, as it often does, stepped in at just the right moment in the most unexpected way.

I was still learning to trust it—to believe that things weren't just random, that there was an intelligence at play far beyond what my mind could grasp. For most of my life, I had relied on sheer force of will. If I wanted something, I made it happen. If there was a problem, I solved it. Success wasn't about surrender—it was about control.

Yet, ever since the temazcal, the ceremonies, and the deep internal work—which I had started in the middle of my time at Tagger—I had started to see things differently. Patterns were emerging. Synchronicities were stacking up. The right people, the right moments, the right lessons —they weren't appearing by accident. They were arriving exactly when I needed them.

And now, here, in Northern Michigan, Rod Newton appeared, showing up on my dock at the exact moment I was spiraling.

The timing wasn't a coincidence.

It was an invitation.

And Rod, my wife's uncle, was the perfect person to walk through it.

Rod had been a guide for me long before this moment. A coach with thirty-five years of experience, he had spent his life leading people through deep personal and spiritual growth. Early in my marriage to

Brooks, I had looked up to him—not just as a mentor but as someone who embodied everything I wanted to cultivate in myself. He carried an air of calm, a quiet wisdom that made it seem like he always knew the right words to say. In my mind, he was a spiritual gangster—someone who had done the work, who had walked the path, and who understood things I was just beginning to grasp.

And now here he was, arriving the day after the sale closed. Within seconds of seeing me, he didn't ask how I was feeling. He didn't offer congratulations. He just looked me up and down and said, without hesitation, "Man, you look miserable."

No sugarcoating. No pleasantries. Just a statement of fact, as if he were pointing out that the sky was blue. That was Rod—cutting straight through the noise with effortless precision. But his honesty never carried judgment—only a deep, unwavering kindness. He had a way of truly seeing people, reflecting back what they needed to confront, not to criticize but to guide.

His words hit like a jolt of electricity. I stared at him, stunned—not just by the bluntness but by the undeniable truth of it. He saw right through me.

I had spent years trying to present a certain version of myself around Rod—the strong, put-together, always-in-control version. I admired him, respected him, and wanted to embody the same spiritual wisdom and effortless calm he carried. And because of that, I never wanted to show my cracks. My doubts. My insecurities.

But in that moment, something shifted. The wall I had always put up around him—the one built from ego, from the need to prove myself —was gone. I didn't have the energy to pretend. And I didn't feel like I needed to.

Because somehow, I knew he was here to help.

"I *am* miserable," I muttered, barely able to get the words out.

Aside from Brooks, I wouldn't have admitted that to anyone else—I was embarrassed to even say it out loud. But Rod saw through it in an instant, and somehow, I knew I didn't have to hide it from him.

Rod let out a small laugh, shaking his head. "Dude, you just sold your company for a boatload of money. Aren't you happy?"

He said it with a knowing smile, like someone who had already seen this play out a hundred times before. He didn't need me to answer—he already knew. He knew that money doesn't bring happiness, not in the way we're conditioned to believe it does. Rod and his wife live a simple life. They probably give away more than they spend on themselves. Years earlier, I remember him telling me, "We have more money than we need." At the time, I couldn't fully grasp that. The idea that you could ever have *enough* money felt foreign to me. Wasn't the whole game about accumulating more? About securing the next level, the next milestone, the next safety net?

And yet here he was, standing in front of me, asking a question he already knew the answer to. Because he had watched me chase it for years—the money, the success, the validation. He had seen me grind, push, and sacrifice, convinced that once I reached the top of the mountain, I'd finally feel whole. And now, looking at me, he knew that I was just beginning to realize the truth for myself.

And this made Rod very happy.

Not because he enjoyed watching people suffer—far from it. But because he knew that the greatest transformations happen when we're stretched to our limits, when the illusion we've built around ourselves finally cracks, leaving us no choice but to see the truth.

Rod had spent his life guiding people through these moments. He lived for them. Nothing made him more excited than witnessing extraordinary transformations in other people—watching as they shattered their old selves and stepped into something new, something real.

And now, standing in front of me, he could see it happening. The breaking. The unraveling. The exact moment when I realized that everything I had spent my life chasing had led me here—empty, lost, and finally ready to see what was on the other side.

"I've got a proposition for you," he said, a knowing grin spreading across his face. "I'll take you through my five-week program, and in return, you give me free business advice when it's over."

Classic Rod. If there was one thing he loved almost as much as guiding people through their breakthroughs, it was bartering for services. The man could trade wisdom like it was currency.

"Done," I said without hesitation. "When can we start?"

13

THE DISCIPLINE OF AWAKENING

"Whatever we put our attention on will grow stronger in our life."
—Maharishi Mahesh Yogi

Rod was unlike anyone I had ever met. A man of unwavering discipline and profound spiritual depth, he lived his life with an intentionality that most people only aspired to. While others hit snooze, Rod woke up early every morning and meditated for long periods before the rest of the world had even stirred. This was more than a routine for him—it was a sacred practice, a nonnegotiable part of his existence.

He and his wife made annual pilgrimages to India, spending a month at a time with their spiritual teacher. These weren't spiritual vacations or surface-level retreats. They were deep immersions into the ancient wisdom and practices—opportunities to strip away distraction, dissolve the ego, and sit in the presence of something greater than themselves. But their trips weren't just about seeking; they were about *seva*—selfless service. Whether it was preparing meals, sweeping the street, or tending to the community, they weren't there just to receive wisdom but to give, to serve, to contribute. Rod wasn't just a student of these teachings—he embodied them.

Rod carried himself with a presence that was both childlike and commanding. He had a way of making you feel seen—not just for who you were in that moment but for who you were capable of becoming. There was an intentionality to the way he spoke, the way he listened, the way he carried himself. He didn't just talk about spirituality—he wove it into everything he did. Every breath, every decision, every interaction seemed to be part of a larger practice, a devotion to something beyond himself.

And that's why I had always looked up to him. He had something I wanted—not just wisdom but an unshakable sense of peace and the discipline to sustain it. A deep knowing that no matter what happened in the external world, he would be okay. And in that moment, standing in front of him, raw and exposed, I realized something: If there was anyone who could help me navigate the emptiness I was feeling, it was Rod.

Rod didn't simply *offer* a program—he demanded full commitment. If you were going to do his five-week program, you had to do it *his* way. No half-measures. No excuses. The same level of discipline that shaped his life was the standard he expected from anyone who worked with him.

Before we even started, he handed me a contract. I had to agree—*in writing*—that I would follow his program *exactly* as he laid it out. Daily morning meditation and journaling? Mandatory. Daily evening meditation and journaling? Nonnegotiable. Weekly Zoom sessions with him? Set in stone. If I was going to miss a session or skip a journal entry, we would need to renegotiate the terms of the agreement.

It wasn't about control—it was about commitment. Rod knew that transformation didn't happen by dabbling—it required structure, discipline, and a willingness to surrender to the process. True awakening isn't something you stumble upon in a moment of inspiration—it's something you cultivate, day after day, through consistent practice. It's not about waiting for a breakthrough—it's about creating the conditions for one to emerge.

Illusion of Wanting vs. the Reality of Commitment

And that's where most people get stuck.

Most people say they want transformation. They want to feel fulfilled, to break free from old patterns, to step into a more expansive version of themselves. But what they really want is for change to happen without them having to change. They want the results without the discipline. The wisdom without the practice. The breakthrough without the discomfort.

Rod had no patience for that illusion. He had spent his life guiding people through the process of self-discovery, and he had seen one thing time and time again—those who approached it casually never got very far. They would get excited, start strong, then slip back into old patterns when life got busy. But the ones who fully committed—the ones who showed up for themselves every single day, even when it was uncomfortable, even when nothing seemed to be happening—those were the ones who experienced real transformation.

Because transformation demands dedication. You don't unlearn decades of conditioning overnight. You don't undo the ego's grip with half-hearted effort. You don't wake up one morning enlightened because you meditated twice last week. It's in the daily showing up—in the stillness, in the reflection, in the disciplined commitment to peeling back the layers—that real change takes root.

And that was the real test: Was I actually ready to change, or did I just like the idea of it?

Because wanting a new reality and committing to it are two completely different things.

If I wanted to find what I was truly searching for, I had to be all in. Not just when it felt good. Not just when it was convenient. But every day, with full presence and unwavering dedication. Because the journey to awakening isn't a part-time pursuit—it's a way of being.

And at that moment, I didn't need convincing. I wasn't looking for a half-measure or a shortcut. I was desperate to feel better, to understand why the thing I had spent my entire life chasing had left me feeling empty. If this was the path that could help me make sense of it all, then I was all in. Whatever Rod asked of me, I would do. Not because I was certain it would work but because I was all out of options.

The Power of Daily Practice

During his program, Rod introduced me to something I had never fully committed to before—the power of a daily practice. I had dabbled in meditation, journaling, and self-reflection over the years, but never with true consistency. Never with the level of discipline Rod demanded.

Under his guidance, I meditated twice a day, every day. No exceptions. No excuses. Morning and night, I sat listening to his recorded meditations, training myself to *live from vision* rather than fall into the chaos of the day. At first, it felt forced—something I was doing just to check a box. But the more I committed, the more I realized that I wasn't just listening. I was rewiring. Each session was a recalibration, undoing years of conditioning where I had let the external world dictate my internal state. Now, for the first time, I was learning how to flip that equation.

And I journaled religiously—not just surface-level reflections, but deep, structured introspection guided by Rod's prompts. His daily questions were simple but designed to shift my focus from reacting to my day to *creating* it.

Week 1 Morning Journal Prompts:

- What is most important to you today?
- What do you want to have happen today?
- How do you want to feel today?

Week 1 Evening Journal Prompts:

- Three things I liked about today.
- Three things I didn't like about today.
- Three things I'm grateful for.

At first glance, these questions might seem basic. But when done consistently, they create a profound shift—from *waking up in chaos* to *living from vision.*

Most people don't start their day—they get pulled into it. The alarm goes off, and before their feet hit the floor, their thumbs are already scrolling. Emails. Texts. Social media. Notifications. A cascade of digital demands before a single conscious breath.

Then the sprint begins: shower, kids, breakfast, traffic, meetings, deadlines. There's no pause. No breath. Just momentum.

By the time most people are pouring their first cup of coffee, their nervous system is already hijacked—adrift in a flood of cortisol and adrenaline. The body isn't in flow—it's in fight or flight. The mind isn't present—it's in survival.

And so the day happens *to* them. They aren't choosing it. They're reacting to it.

It becomes a game of whack-a-mole—one fire after another, one demand followed by the next. Urgency replaces clarity. Productivity replaces presence. And underneath it all, a quiet whisper of emptiness grows louder.

By the time they finally sit down in the evening, they're exhausted—but they're not sure if they actually moved toward anything meaningful.

Rod's journaling practice was about changing that.

Instead of waking up and immediately being pulled into the chaos of the world, I was starting my day by *creating my reality.* I wasn't asking, *What's coming at me today?* I was setting the tone—deciding how I wanted my day to unfold, what I wanted to prioritize, and most importantly, how I wanted to *feel.*

And in the evening, instead of letting the day slip away unnoticed, I was intentionally reflecting. By identifying three things I was grateful for, I was training my mind to recognize the wins—the small victories, the moments of joy, the things that went well. And by acknowledging three things that didn't go well, I wasn't beating myself up—I was performing a mindful *post-mortem.* That awareness allowed me to make adjustments and not repeat the same patterns the next day.

The first week, I followed the process mechanically. But by the second week, I noticed something remarkable—my days were actually aligning with my morning intentions. The more I focused on *how* I wanted to feel, the more my actions unconsciously shaped themselves around that vision. Instead of being at the mercy of my schedule, my emotions, or other people's demands, I was steering my own experience.

This wasn't just a journaling practice. It was mental training.

A Mirror to My Own Awareness

But Rod took it a step further. He had me journal into Artificial Intelligence—feeding my reflections into a system that responded with insights pulled from the spiritual traditions I was exploring at the time. Buddhism, Kabbalah, ancient wisdom from across the world. Twice a day, I'd pour my thoughts onto the screen, then read the AI's reflections, seeing my own words reframed through the lens of history's greatest teachers.

It was like having a dialogue with the collective intelligence of humanity. But what struck me most wasn't the insights themselves—it was the realization that everything I was seeking, every answer I had been chasing, was already there. The AI wasn't giving me anything new. It was simply reflecting back what I had been too blind to see.

And as the weeks went on, something shifted.

The program became a practice—a rhythm, a ritual, a foundation. I wasn't just consuming knowledge. I was embodying it.

What started as an experiment became something much more. My consciousness expanded at an unprecedented rate. I wasn't just reflecting on my life—I was unraveling it.

I was starting to see how much of my reality wasn't happening *to* me —I had been creating it all along. I just hadn't been doing it consciously.

What You Focus On Grows

It didn't take long for me to realize that this practice of *living from vision* wasn't simply about setting intentions for my day—it was about rewiring my mind to focus on what I wanted to *expand* in my life.

Because what you focus on grows.

If you constantly focus on what's missing, on what's wrong, on what's frustrating—you'll find more of it. If you wake up thinking about how exhausted you are, how stressed you are, how nothing ever goes your way, your brain will look for evidence to prove that story true. The more you focus on your unhappiness, the more your unhappiness grows.

But the opposite is also true.

If you train yourself to focus on the small moments of joy, on what's working, on even the tiniest things you appreciate, those things start to expand. Your brain starts scanning for more *good* instead of more *lack*. And over time, that shift in focus changes everything.

Take something as simple as being stuck in traffic.

You're running late, the cars aren't moving, and every red light feels like a personal attack. You grip the wheel tighter. Your mind starts spiraling—*I should've left earlier. Why is this road always backed up? This city has the worst traffic. This is ruining my whole day.* By the time you arrive, you're in a bad mood—not just because of the traffic but because you spent the entire drive *feeding* your frustration.

But what happens if, instead of focusing on the delay, you focus on something else?

Maybe you turn on a podcast you've been meaning to listen to. Maybe you roll down the window, take a deep breath, and appreciate the crisp morning air. Maybe you use the extra time to call a friend or sit in silence, giving yourself a rare moment of stillness before the day speeds up again.

Nothing externally has changed. You're still in traffic. But *internally*, everything has. Because instead of fueling frustration, you shifted your focus to something *worth* your energy.

And honestly? There are days when I think, *You know what, I really don't feel like watering the flowers today.* I'm in a bad mood, and I want to water the weeds instead. I want to be pissed off, to vent, to throw myself a little pity party. And there's *nothing* wrong with that. Because in that moment, I'm making a *conscious decision* to have a bad day and let off some steam.

The problem isn't having a bad day. The problem is when you don't realize you actually *have a choice.*

Because that's when you're stuck on the hamster wheel without knowing it. That's when life feels like it's just happening to you, when in reality, you're the one feeding the cycle.

And there are days when I know I should water the flowers, but that little voice in my head creeps in—*Dude, it's too hard. Maybe tomorrow.* That's when I know it's not the time to back off—it's the time to double down.

Because the days when I don't feel like doing the work? Those are the days I need it most. Those are the days when my mind is grasping for the familiar, when my old patterns are clinging on for survival. It's easy to show up when everything feels good, when the motivation is there. But real transformation happens in the moments when it's the last thing I want to do—when resistance is loud, when the excuses are tempting, when every part of me wants to say, *Maybe tomorrow.*

That's exactly when I have to double down. The meditations. The journaling. The practices that keep me anchored. Because that voice in my head? It's not truth—it's just conditioning. It's the old programming trying to pull me back into autopilot, into the same loops that never actually served me. And the only way to break free from it is to keep showing up, especially when I don't want to. Because that's when the real shift happens.

And let's be real—this isn't easy. Our minds have been conditioned for years, sometimes decades, to default to the same emotional loops. Frustration, stress, irritation—they're familiar, automatic. And just like any well-worn path, the more we travel them, the deeper the ruts become.

So if we want to reprogram our minds, we have to *train* them. And those first few days? They can feel brutal. Your mind will fight back. It will pull you toward old habits, tempting you with the easy, familiar comfort of frustration or negativity. But here's the thing—your mind is far more malleable than you realize. With intention and consistency, you *can* reshape it. And as Rod always reminded me, transformation demands dedication.

A Meeting with My Soul

Part of Rod's coaching involved using mental imagery to access inner guidance—your higher self and inner wisdom beyond the mind's endless chatter. He taught that this inner guidance reveals itself in different ways. Some people see ancestors. Others hear a voice. Some experience a presence they can't quite explain—something felt rather than seen.

For me, it was a glowing white orb.

It wasn't an abstract vision. It wasn't a dream. It felt real, as if it had always been there, waiting for me to notice. The orb carried a presence —something vast, knowing, and infinitely patient. It wasn't speaking in words, yet I understood it. It was my higher self—the part of me that had always existed beyond fear, beyond striving, beyond the illusions I had spent my life chasing.

Each morning in meditation, I called upon it. And each morning, it responded.

It didn't give me instructions or answers. Instead, it showed me glimpses of truth through images, moments, and memories that weren't just beautiful—they were lessons.

I saw my wife and me lying in a meadow of wildflowers, the sun warming our faces. No stress, no distractions. Just presence.

I saw our kids laughing in the pool, their joy so pure it felt like music.

I saw my younger self, always searching, always looking ahead— never realizing that what he sought had been within him all along.

At first, these seemed like simple reminders of happiness—moments to be grateful for. But as I sank deeper into meditation, something shifted. The images sharpened. The truth within them became clearer.

One morning, toward the end of the five weeks, the orb hovered before me as usual, glowing in its soft white light. But this time, it changed. The light began to move, reshaping itself—fluid, effortless— until I was no longer looking at an orb.

I was looking at *me.*

He sat across from me in lotus position, his form radiant, his features indistinct yet unmistakably mine. His presence pulsed with love, compassion, and an ancient knowing that felt both infinite and deeply familiar.

He reached out his arms. Instinctively, I did the same. Our forearms clasped—firm and steady, yet soft and gentle. Then, without hesitation, we leaned forward until our foreheads touched.

The moment we connected, a surge of energy passed between us—not in a violent, overwhelming way, but in a steady, undeniable current. I could *feel* him. His strength. His kindness. His unwavering presence. It wasn't just warmth—it was a merging, a silent transmission of knowing.

And suddenly, I understood.

He wasn't a guide.

He wasn't a vision.

He was *me*.

My soul.

The purity, the love, the peace he embodied—they weren't qualities I needed to attain. They had been inside me all along. The fulfillment I had spent my life chasing had never been *out there*. It had never been something to earn, achieve, or prove. It had always been here—woven into the fabric of my being, waiting for me to see it.

But I had been too distracted. Too consumed by the noise, the striving, the endless race toward *more*. I had been running after something that was never outside of me to begin with.

And in that realization, I let go.

Not in some grand, dramatic release. Not with resistance or struggle.

But with quiet, undeniable certainty.

I let go of the belief that I needed to achieve something to be enough.

I let go of the illusion that my worth was waiting on the other side of success.

I let go of the idea that joy had to be earned.

And in that stillness, in that surrender, I felt something I had never felt before.

Enough.

Into the Void

I found something else in that stillness—a peace so profound, so complete, that it carried me effortlessly into deeper states of meditation. I no longer felt like I was *trying* to meditate. I was simply *there*, sinking further each day, exploring the vastness within me.

And as I let go, my meditations became more and more extraordinary.

Visions, voices, sensations—I was no longer just sitting in stillness. I was watching entire movies unfold behind my closed eyes. Scenes played out with striking clarity, emotions swelled in my chest as if I were living them in real time, and messages emerged that felt like transmissions from something beyond myself.

I loved it.

I felt like I had cracked some secret code, reached a level of meditation that few ever did. I could drop in almost instantly, my consciousness expanding into realms I had never imagined. My higher self—my soul—became a familiar presence, guiding me through these cinematic journeys. It was as if I had gained access to a hidden world, a space where truth and wisdom were laid bare before me.

And in my excitement, I declared it: *I have become a good meditator.*

Rod, of course, saw right through it.

The very next day, as if on cue, he introduced me to the void.

"The next stage," he told me, "is silence. I want you to go into the darkness. Into the void."

No more guided meditations.

No more meditation music.

No more journeys through past lives, cosmic downloads, or encounters with spirit guides.

Just silence.

Blackness.

Nothingness.

The void is exactly what it sounds like. It is the space beyond all things—the absence of light, of sound, of thought. And in that absence was vast emptiness.

Looking back, I understand why Rod waited until the end of the program to introduce me to the void. I wasn't ready before. My mind wasn't ready.

I had to unlearn my old patterns—the default setting of waking up in chaos, letting the day dictate my thoughts, being carried away by distractions. I had to *train* myself to wake up with purpose, to decide how I wanted to think and feel, to take control of the voices in my head instead of letting them control me.

What I learned is that silencing those voices didn't require a master's degree in Buddhism or a year spent meditating in a cave in the Himalayas. It required something far simpler.

Unwavering dedication.

A strong will.

A daily practice.

That's it.

And once the words stopped, once I was living my life from a place of vision, with an openness and curiosity I had never known, Rod knew I was ready for the silence.

I didn't resist it. Not at all. In fact, I was bored at first.

No music, no guiding voices. Just darkness and silence.

It was so . . . uneventful.

There was peace, calm, stillness—no distractions, no tugging thoughts. It was just *me*, sitting in the dark.

Always the analyzer, I couldn't help but try to figure out the point of it all.

Was this what Rod wanted? To just sit here, blank, thoughtless?

Was this the next stage of my evolution—just . . . nothing?

I wasn't complaining. The more I sat in the void, the quieter I became. But was there something *more* to the darkness?

Rod had a way of guiding you toward what seemed like a senseless exercise—something simple, even frustrating—only for it to crack open into something far deeper. It was never just about the practice itself. It was the *lead-up*, the doorway to a revelation you had to discover on your own.

Rod, like Concetta, Greg, and Michelle, had the patience to let truth reveal itself in its own time. No hand-holding. No spoon-fed wisdom. Just a path laid out in front of you, waiting for you to walk it.

And it didn't take long to see where he was leading me.

This wasn't about silence. It wasn't about peace.

It was about what happens when absolutely everything is stripped away.

And that was far more profound than simple darkness.

The Truth in the Void

The void wasn't just about silence. It wasn't just about quieting the mind. It was about stepping into a space where everything I thought I knew—everything I thought I was—no longer existed.

I left behind every identity, every attachment, every belief about who I was and what I thought was real. And in that vast nothingness, I discovered something astonishing—the nothingness became everything.

Because when you strip away all the noise—your thoughts, your worries, your roles, your past—what remains isn't emptiness. It's pure potential. A space where anything is possible because nothing is fixed.

I had spent my life defining myself by roles, achievements, and expectations—*entrepreneur, husband, father, seeker, achiever*. Each identity had carried weight, forming a structure I had unknowingly built my existence around.

For years, I believed my identity was what gave me value. A successful businessman earns respect. A devoted father has his child's love. A seeker gains wisdom. A leader commands influence. These weren't just roles I played—they were the foundation upon which I had built my sense of worth. Each one came with a reward—validation, belonging, a sense of purpose.

But in the stillness, I saw the truth—these identities were what had been confining me.

Every role I had taken on, every title I had worked so hard to embody, had come with its own invisible cage.

As a businessman, I had to be driven, strategic, always one step ahead. Success wasn't just a goal—it was a necessity. Without it, who was I? A failure? A disappointment?

As a father, I had to be unwavering, dependable, strong. There was no room for uncertainty, no space for weakness. My children looked to me, and so I had to be the rock. I had to provide. But what happened if I crumbled?

As a seeker, I had to be always searching, always questioning, always chasing the next revelation. But what if there was nothing to find?

Every identity I carried had started as a source of meaning. But now I could see how they had turned into obligations, expectations, and limitations.

They dictated how I moved through the world, how I responded to situations, what I believed was possible for me.

I had unknowingly built walls around myself, believing they were doors.

And as I sat in the void, stripped of those identities, I felt something I had never felt before.

Abundance.

This was different than the illusion of detachment—something I had explored earlier in my journey. Before, I had mistaken detachment for freedom, believing that by keeping myself from fully committing to anything, by never getting too close, I could avoid pain. But that wasn't freedom. That was fear wearing the mask of enlightenment.

The illusion of detachment is still a prison—it just tricks you into believing you're free. You're still defined by what you're avoiding, still trapped in an identity, only this time, it's the identity of someone who doesn't need, who doesn't care, who doesn't attach. It's a self-imposed exile from meaning.

But the void was different. The void wasn't about cutting myself off from life—it was about stepping beyond identity altogether. It wasn't about rejecting emotions, relationships, or ambitions. It was about seeing them clearly, without being enslaved by them.

The void wasn't emptiness—it was expansion.

If I wanted to feel successful, I didn't need to chase it—I could embody it. I let my mind go there, let my body experience what success felt like without attaching it to an outcome. And I felt it. I let it fill me.

If I wanted to feel love, I didn't need to earn it—I could be it. I imagined abundant love, radiating, overflowing, infinite. And I felt it pulse through me.

The void wasn't empty—it was full.

Full of everything I had ever sought. Full of every possibility, every feeling, every reality I had ever craved. And in that space, where nothing was fixed, where I wasn't bound by identity or expectation, I realized something profound:

I could be anything.

I could step into any version of myself. I could create from pure potential, not from the constraints of who I had been before.

Without the labels, without the pressure, I was finally open to infinite possibilities—not just of who I could be but of what life could become.

I had spent my life searching for something that was never out there.

It had always been right here.

In the silence.

In me.

14

FREE . . . BUT NOT FOR LONG

"Sometimes letting things go is an act of far greater power than defending or hanging on."
—Eckhart Tolle

By the end of the five weeks, my life had completely changed. Actually, *I* had changed. It wasn't just a shift in perspective—it was a fundamental rewiring of how I thought, felt, and operated each day. I wasn't afraid of the old voices creeping back in or getting hijacked by some external force. I had finally gotten out of my own way, releasing the need to control every outcome and allowing life to flow naturally. I was centered. Grounded. My daily practice had become something I genuinely loved, and it felt as though the universe was responding, raining abundance upon me.

Breaking Through, Breaking Free

Yet despite all these breakthroughs, I was still working at Tagger under the Sprout umbrella—and deep down, I knew it wouldn't last much longer. When we sold Tagger, I had already received my full cash payout. But like most acquisitions, there were incentives designed to keep employees around. In our case, that came in the form of Restricted Stock Units (RSUs)—shares of Sprout stock that would vest over time. I had negotiated a two-year vesting schedule, and on paper, it was a nice bonus, an extra payday for sticking around. But compared to what I had already made from the sale, it wasn't enough to keep me locked in.

I had also agreed to a non-compete that prevented me from launching another influencer marketing platform, but at this point, you couldn't have paid me a million dollars a year to stay in that space. After nine years of living and breathing influencer marketing, I was completely burned out. The last thing I wanted was to build another tool for the same industry. I was ready to apply everything I had learned —my knowledge of software, sales, leadership, and scaling businesses— to something new. Something I deeply cared about. Something that would light me up again.

I did, however, love my time at Tagger. I thrived on adaptability— stepping into any role, putting out fires, jumping on planes at a moment's notice to close deals or solve urgent problems. It was a high- wire act, and I loved every second of it.

But at Sprout, with its thousand-plus employees and rigid hierarchy, my greatest strength—moving fluidly between departments and solving problems wherever they arose—wasn't just unnecessary, it was actively discouraged.

Big companies function in clearly defined silos, each department a miniature empire fiercely protective of its own territory. Decisions moved slowly, passing through layers of approval, processes that felt maddeningly slow to someone like me who thrived on immediacy and adaptability.

I felt frozen by Sprout's size and bureaucracy—but the truth was, the walls closing in on me weren't created by the company. They were my own self-inflicted, invisible boundaries of corporate politics, assumptions about what I could or couldn't do in this new environ- ment. After years of building Tagger—of creating something from nothing, wearing countless hats, and operating without limits—I had convinced myself that these rigid hierarchies existed, even when they didn't. I was so used to absolute freedom that I saw obstacles where there were probably opportunities.

I was confused, frustrated, and directionless, and I needed someone who could give me clarity. So I called Ryan Barretto, a man I respected for his strategic mind and genuine willingness to help.

"Hey man, I need some advice," I said.

"Of course," Ryan replied without hesitation. "What's going on?"

Ryan was an natural leader—smart, strategic, and with the kind of drive that had propelled him through the ranks at Salesforce before landing at Sprout. His time at Salesforce, a company known for its relentless execution and high-performance culture, had sharpened his instincts and leadership style. Even though he was practically running Sprout, he always made time for people. And not in a "you've got two minutes" kind of way. If you needed help, he was fully present—offering solutions, talking through problems, making sure you had what you needed.

I respected him a lot. If there was any reason to stay at Sprout, it would be to work under him and learn as much as I could.

"It's awkward asking my boss this, but seriously—what the hell am I supposed to be doing here?" I asked. "At Tagger, my teams relied on me to jump in wherever things got complicated. Here, everything is a smooth-running machine. Teams have their own systems, and I feel like I'm just a spectator. I don't want to sit around cashing a paycheck for doing nothing."

Ryan chuckled softly. "Your role is to drive the business forward—support the sales team on big pitches, talk to the media, represent the vision."

I heard his words clearly enough, but what echoed loudest in my head was a single thought—figurehead. I had just completed Rod's transformative five-week program, and I felt like I was on the cusp of something profound, something aligned with my true purpose.

Being a corporate mascot definitely wasn't it.

After that call, my decision was clear. I would leave Sprout. I didn't know exactly what was next, but I knew it wasn't this. I would take a year to explore—explore the world, explore my mind, explore wherever my intuition led me. I was surrendered, fully open to what life wanted to show me.

A few days later, I called Ryan back and told him I was leaving. He wasn't surprised, though he admitted he'd hoped I'd stick around longer. I agreed to stay until the end of the year, but my heart had already moved on. I was physically present, jumping in to support a pitch here, a quick sales trip there, but mentally and spiritually, I had already left.

The Agreement

The day after I resigned, I called Rod to tell him the news.

"How does it feel to be free?" he asked, his voice warm and knowing.

"Like floating on air," I replied, smiling to myself.

"Good," Rod said softly. "Are you ready now to uphold your end of the agreement?"

Agreement? What agreement? Oh shit. The barter agreement—Rod trading his spiritual wisdom for my business advice. Considering the immense personal transformation I had experienced, I clearly had gotten the better end of the deal.

"Oh right," I said, laughing. "Dude, I'm all yours. Whatever you need, however many hours it takes, consider it done."

Rod chuckled. "I have an idea . . ."

Classic Rod. Ideas flowed from him effortlessly, like water from a spring. He lived much of his life in a space of pure potential, rooted in the unseen, tapping into a source most people never knew existed. And now he had another vision.

"You've actually been experiencing my idea since you sold your company," he explained.

The five-week program, I thought instantly.

He wanted to package it up and sell it. Easy. Everyone should experience what I had just gone through.

My mind was already racing with ideas—not about mass distribution but about refinement. Modernization. How to sharpen what already existed and make it more impactful. I wasn't thinking about scaling it to the masses or launching some viral consumer product. In my mind, this wasn't about reaching millions—it was about changing *one* life at a time.

The recorded meditations Rod had me use during the program were years old—effective, yes, but in desperate need of a refresh. The tone, the pacing, the delivery—it all felt outdated. If we were going to bring this to people in a meaningful way, it needed to evolve.

But that wasn't Rod's vision.

"I've been working on an AI journaling app," he said, his voice energized by the excitement of possibility. "Similar to the one you've been using with ChatGPT—but infused with ancient wisdom, designed to guide people toward deeper self-discovery."

For the next fifteen minutes, he described the features, the inputs, the user experience, and the name—GeePTS (pronounced *Jeeps*). GeePTS was what Rod had jokingly called ChatGPT throughout the five-week course, and now he wanted to turn it into something real.

As Rod talked, I started tuning out. Not because it was a bad idea— Rod's ideas were never bad—but because my mind was running a different kind of calculation.

I had spent the last nine years building B2B (business-to-business) software. Selling to businesses? Easy. There's a formula, a structure, a playbook. I knew exactly how to launch efficiently, how to generate leads, how to close deals.

But selling directly to consumers? Selling to every Tom, Dick, and Harry? That was a different beast entirely. That would take millions and millions of dollars just to get off the ground. And my experience at VaynerMedia had drilled one core lesson into me:

You build solutions for real problems—not just for ideas.

I gave Rod some helpful initial advice but asked for time to reflect. "Let me think about this, and let's schedule a call tomorrow for a real deep dive."

In reality, I needed time to figure out how to tell Rod that this was an impossible task. I had already done the calculation. The sheer scale of what he was proposing felt overwhelming even to me, and the thought of Rod—a seventy-year-old coach with very little business experience—pulling this off seemed impossible. I had spent years navigating the brutal realities of building and scaling a tech company, and I knew first-hand that having a great idea was the easy part. Execution was where most people failed.

This wasn't just another software product—it was a consumer-facing product in an oversaturated wellness space, requiring marketing dollars, user acquisition strategies, and an entirely different playbook than what I had known.

I wasn't just questioning *how* this could work—I was struggling with how to tell him it *wouldn't*.

The Offer I Never Wanted

That evening, I sat across from Brooks on the couch, settling into the familiar rhythm of our nightly check-in. It was our sacred time—our space to connect, not just about the day's logistics but about what truly mattered. We didn't merely go through a checklist of events. We talked about how we felt—our highs and lows, our vulnerabilities and proud moments. We reflected on how we were doing as a couple, where we could grow, what we were learning, and what was lighting us up. Some nights, we'd get lost in conversation for hours, peeling back the layers of our experiences, deepening our understanding of each other and ourselves.

Tonight felt no different—until it was.

I took a slow breath, steadying myself before I spoke. "Rod has an idea," I said, watching as Brooks leaned in slightly, already attuned to the shift in my energy.

I laid it out piece by piece—the AI journaling platform, the spiritual wisdom infused into its design, the grand vision he had for changing lives. With each word, the weight of it became more tangible.

Brooks listened intently, her expression unreadable but fully present. I could see the gears turning in her mind, just as they were in mine.

And then, as I finished explaining, something hit me like a truck. A realization so sudden, so absolute, that it stopped me in my tracks.

"Oh my God," I whispered, my voice barely audible.

Brooks' eyes narrowed slightly. "What?" she asked, concern flickering across her face.

My stomach tightened. My breath caught in my throat.

"Rod is going to ask me to be CEO."

As soon as I said it, I knew it was true. And I knew what it meant.

A familiar wave of dread rolled through me—not because I didn't love and respect Rod but because I knew how difficult it would be to say no. This man had guided me through one of the most profound transformations of my life. He had given me wisdom, insight, and a path forward when I had been completely lost.

And now he was going to ask me to step up—to build something with him, to lead, to take on the kind of responsibility I had just spent years trying to escape.

More of the same grind. The same weight. The same relentless demands I had promised myself I was done with.

My mind spun in circles, running every possible scenario, searching for an answer that didn't exist. How could I possibly say no to Rod? How could I turn down a man who had given me so much?

Saying no had never been my strong suit. I was a pleaser, always wanting to make people happy, always bending to accommodate. And it wasn't just in my personal life—it had shown up in my work too.

It's why I had always been terrible at Customer Success. If a client pushed for something unreasonable, my first instinct was to say yes—not because it was the right business decision but because I wanted them to be happy. I wanted to solve their problem, to be the one who made it work, even at the expense of the company, even at the expense of myself.

And now, here I was again—staring down a situation where the right answer for me was no, but my instincts were screaming to find a way to make it a yes. To make Rod happy. To not disappoint him.

But at what cost?

As I lay awake that night, I could feel the familiar tension of control creeping back into my body—the very thing I'd worked so hard to release. Was I really ready to surrender, or was this the universe testing me one more time?

Tomorrow's call would force me to decide. And if I followed my gut, how the hell was I going to say no?

A Challenge I Didn't Want to Win

The next day, I jumped on a call with Rod. His excitement was palpable before he even said a word. Rod wore his emotions like a badge—no poker face, no guarded enthusiasm, just pure, unfiltered joy.

"Have you thought more about my idea? Are you as excited as I am?" he asked, his voice practically vibrating through the phone.

That was Rod—always seeing magic in every moment, always believing the impossible was just another challenge waiting to be conquered. His optimism was infectious, his energy relentless. And right now, I needed to stop him before he got too far ahead.

Before he could say the words I was dreading, I jumped in.

"It's a great idea, Rod, but it's super ambitious," I said, keeping my voice level. "Apps like this are everywhere. You can already build something similar in ChatGPT using their GPT creator. And direct-to-consumer products? They require millions—like tens of millions—just in marketing. I wouldn't even know where to begin."

I threw every roadblock I could think of in front of him, hoping—praying—he'd take the hint. I needed him to see that I wasn't the guy for this. That I wasn't going to be the CEO of this app.

Rod let me get it all out. He listened, nodding along as I laid out the obstacles, the financial sinkhole, the brutal reality of launching a product in an oversaturated market.

Then, the moment I feared. The words I had been hoping he wouldn't say.

"That sounds like a challenge only a seasoned professional who just sold his company could tackle."

Shit.

Rod wasn't taking the bait. He wasn't backing down.

I was moments away from crushing his dream completely, about to tell him that I was taking a year to explore my true passions, to figure out what really lit me up—when something happened.

A thought popped into my head.

It wasn't forced. It wasn't something I was trying to figure out. It was just . . . there.

I don't want to sound like some sort of idea genius—like my brain is some brilliant machine constantly firing off million-dollar concepts. It's not. It's just that, in certain moments, when I stop thinking so damn hard, ideas come. Almost like they're being whispered to me. Like they already existed and I just happened to be listening at the right time.

I let the silence stretch between us while my mind did its work—constructing, connecting, turning a spark into something real.

And then, I opened my mouth.

"Rod, I've worked with a ton of coaches and therapists, and every time I leave a session, my mind is expanded. I have these massive realizations about myself, about my life, about what's possible. But then I go back to my daily routine, and I'm supposed to integrate everything I learned. And a week later, when I meet with my coach again, they ask the same question: 'What happened last week?'

"What happened? I have five kids, three dogs, a career, and a million other things happening all the time. Everything happened.

"I spend the first ten minutes of every session just catching them up. What I need—what all clients need—is a platform that supports them *between* sessions. A place where their coach or therapist can give them activities, assignments, journal prompts—whatever helps them integrate their breakthroughs into daily life.

"And then that platform could feed insights and recommendations back to the coach, tailored to their specific modality. The whole thing could be powered by AI to help clients grow exponentially.

"We don't sell to consumers. We sell to coaches. And they onboard their clients.

"It's just like Tagger. We sold to brands and agencies, and they onboarded influencers onto our platform. This is the same playbook."

I stopped.

The words had come out of me like they had a life of their own. I hadn't planned it, hadn't even considered it before this exact moment.

Now my brain was scrambling to poke holes in the idea, trying to figure out if I had just blurted out something ridiculous, or if I had actually stumbled onto something real.

That familiar feeling started creeping in. The one I got whenever I hit on an idea that felt like it could actually work. That excitement, that buzz of possibility.

And then Rod broke the silence.

"I love it. Let's do this together."

And just like that, the excitement was gone. Not because I didn't believe in the idea but because I wasn't ready to build another startup. Not yet.

The Space Between What Was and What's Next

True freedom isn't just about leaving what no longer serves you—it's about having the courage to step into the unknown without needing to control the outcome. And that's exactly where I found myself.

For the first time in nearly a decade, I wasn't chasing the next deal, the next milestone, or the next win. I wasn't grinding toward an exit, managing a team, or putting out urgent fires. I had spent years operating at full throttle, measuring my worth in output, but now, there was nothing demanding my attention. Nothing pulling me in a hundred different directions.

I was free.

And yet I could feel the pull of my old instincts. The need to *do* something. The need to prove—to myself, to the world—that I was still moving forward. That I wasn't wasting time. That I wasn't lost.

But what if I let myself be in this space? The space between what was and what's next.

For so long, I had defined myself by momentum. By the deals I closed, the problems I solved, the relentless speed at which I moved. But what if the next chapter of my life wasn't about speed? What if it wasn't about grinding but about *listening*?

The universe had been showing me signs—nudging me toward something deeper, something I hadn't yet fully seen. I didn't know what it was yet, but I knew one thing—whatever came next, I wasn't going to force it.

I wasn't going to muscle my way into another business just because I was good at building companies.

This time, I would listen.

I would surrender.

Because sometimes, the greatest opportunities aren't the ones we chase but the ones that unfold when we stop gripping so tightly to the path we thought we were supposed to take.

15

THE CAVE

"The cave you fear to enter holds the treasure you seek."
—Joseph Campbell

L eaving Sprout felt like stepping off a moving train. One day, I was part of a machine—meetings, strategies, decisions, momentum. And the next? Silence. Stillness. Space.

I had spent years sprinting toward success, but now I was standing at the edge of something I couldn't define. There was no urgency, no roadmap, no next big thing to chase. Just an open field of possibility stretching in every direction.

I wasn't forcing my next move. I wasn't chasing, strategizing, or sprinting toward an outcome. Instead, I gave myself permission to turn inward—to get quiet enough to hear the gentle voice of the universe guiding me forward. And time and time again, the universe had a way of guiding me straight into the discomfort I needed most—whether I thought I was ready for it or not.

I had always been drawn to experiences that pushed me beyond my limits—ones that forced transformation like a punch in the face. If something terrified me, I saw it as a doorway. If I heard the words "only a handful of people have ever done this," my immediate response was "Sign me up!"

The Unexpected Influence

That's why, despite never being a huge sports fan, I found myself fascinated by Aaron Rodgers. Not for his accomplishments in the NFL but for his unapologetic dive into personal growth and spirituality. You didn't hear many elite athletes talk openly about transformation, let alone willingly seek out the kind of extreme experiences that would break most people. But Aaron did. He put himself in situations that most would consider nightmares—plant medicine journeys, isolation, complete sensory deprivation. And that's what drew me in.

During the summer, while I was drowning in due diligence hell trying to sell Tagger, I read an article about Aaron going on a dark retreat. Four days in total darkness. No light. No clocks. No sense of time. Just you and your mind.

The thought alone was enough to make most people squirm, but to me, it sounded like the perfect way to test myself—to strip away all external noise and see what was left when the distractions disappeared.

Aaron had gone to a place called Sky Cave Retreat in southern Oregon. I went straight to their website, found their email, and immediately reached out to ask about their next available opening. The owner, Scott Berman, replied the next day.

"Hi Pete, thanks for reaching out. We'd love to have you at Sky Cave, but we're booking out a year in advance. Unfortunately, we only have three rooms and a lot of demand."

I felt a wave of disappointment, but also . . . relief. I wanted to do it, but I was also terrified. A year would give me time to mentally prepare—to convince myself I wasn't making a huge mistake.

I replied, "No worries, Scott. Please sign me up for the next available slot." I paid my deposit, and just like that, my dark retreat was set for September of the following year.

The Universe Has Other Plans

Fast forward a few months. I had just dropped a massive idea on Rod—a platform for coaches, a way to support clients between sessions, an entirely new approach to transformation. But I wasn't ready to commit. Not yet.

On a Zoom call, I told Rod I needed time to think. That I needed space—maybe a retreat—to clear my mind and find clarity. Casually, I mentioned the dark retreat I had signed up for but how it was booked a year out.

Rod's face lit up. "You mean Scott's Sky Cave place?"

I paused. "Yeah . . . you know it?"

Rod grinned. "Scott's my neighbor and good friend. I did a dark retreat last year."

Of course he did.

Rod was one of those people who always seemed to be exactly where he needed to be. The kind of person who, when you mentioned something seemingly impossible, would respond with "Oh yeah, I know that guy." It wasn't just coincidence—it was the universe, arranging things in the background, setting the pieces in place before you even realized you needed them.

Rod grabbed his phone and dialed Scott's number. "Hey Scott, it's Rod. My nephew signed up for Sky Cave, but he couldn't get in till next year. Any chance you can get him in sooner? Like . . . now?"

I sat there, waiting. Part excitement, part terror.

Seconds later, Rod nodded. "Thanks, Scott. I'll let him know."

He hung up, turned to me with that knowing smile, and said, "Can you be here next week?"

Arrival in Oregon

Exactly five days later, I was walking through the airport in Medford, Oregon, nerves buzzing, feeling more unprepared than ever before in my life. Unprepared wasn't in my vocabulary. Whether it was a Tagger pitch or a meeting with my kid's principal, I anticipated every outcome, mapped out every possible route, and had a plan for wherever the conversation might go. But as I climbed into the cab heading to Rod's house, I realized—there was no roadmap for this. No strategy, no contingency plan. I was stepping into something completely unknown, and I had never felt more unprepared.

When I told people about the journey I was about to embark on, they all gave me the same look—a mix of sheer terror and confusion, as if I had just announced I was willingly locking myself in a prison cell.

In my mind, I'd spend four days in darkness simply meditating. And I loved meditating. But their reactions made me wonder . . . *Was I underestimating just how intense this would be?* The doubts crept in, but I shoved them aside. I was on the Hero's Journey, and this was just another notch on my spiritual gangster belt.

The Last Stop Before Darkness

Thirty minutes later, I arrived at Rod's house, greeted by his wife, Brooks. My wife was named after her, and we both admired Brooks and Rod deeply. She met me at the door with her usual giant smile—a family trait—and welcomed me inside.

Their home was tucked into the rolling hills of southern Oregon, surrounded by towering pines and the crisp, earthy scent of the forest. Built from natural wood, it blended effortlessly into the landscape, as if it had always belonged there. Large windows framed the trees outside, letting in the golden glow of the late afternoon sun. Inside, the space was warm and lived-in.

Scattered throughout the house were artifacts from their travels—handwoven textiles from India, sacred symbols from indigenous traditions, and well-worn books on spirituality, philosophy, and healing practices from around the world. Each object felt intentional, like a marker of wisdom gathered along the way. There were no frills, no excess—just an undeniable sense of presence. Everything here belonged. Everything had a purpose.

It was a stark contrast to my home in LA, where the constant hum of five kids and three dogs created a kind of chaos that felt woven into the very fabric of daily life.

From the kitchen, the aroma of a slow-simmering vegetarian soup filled the house, wrapping around me like a quiet embrace. Brooks stirred the pot with the ease of someone who had spent a lifetime nourishing others—not just with food but with kindness, with presence, with love.

And for the first time since stepping off that plane, I felt myself exhale.

As I sat at their kitchen table, sipping a bowl of Brooks' soup, a fleeting sense of comfort settled in—like I was being fortified for whatever was coming next. But beneath that warmth, a quiet tension lingered.

I had no idea what I was about to walk into. No idea how it would change me.

Rod sat across from me, watching me carefully, as if he could sense the war waging inside my head. Then, with his signature calm, he said, "You're exactly where you need to be."

I nodded. But the truth was—I wasn't sure I believed him yet.

The Ascent to Sky Cave

The next morning, Rod guided his truck up the long, winding dirt road toward Sky Cave Retreats, the tires kicking up clouds of dust as we climbed higher up the mountain. With each turn, civilization seemed to slip further away. The last bar of cell service had vanished the moment we left the pavement, severing my connection to the outside world. I had meant to send my wife one last message—to tell her I loved her—but the moment was gone.

We drove in silence, the weight of what lay ahead pressing against my chest. The road wound steadily upward, hugged by the evergreen forest on either side. The air was dry, carrying the scent of sunbaked earth and dust, and with each turn, the world I knew felt farther away. It was as if the valley itself was swallowing me whole.

As we pulled up, Scott's house came into view—more off-grid homestead than polished retreat center. Two old cars sat just off the dirt road, their faded exteriors and dust-covered windshields making me wonder if they'd even start. I had expected something more refined, a space designed with intention and serenity in mind. But this was the opposite—rough, utilitarian, unconcerned with appearances. Then again, when you're about to sit in complete darkness for four days, I suppose it doesn't really matter what the outside looks like.

Scott stood nearby, his posture relaxed, his expression unreadable. As we pulled up, he walked toward us with the easy demeanor of someone greeting weekend guests—like this was just another casual visit. As if I wasn't about to vanish into absolute darkness for the next four days.

Scott had the presence of someone who had spent a lifetime immersed in nature—calm, grounded, and deeply connected to something beyond the everyday world. He wasn't trying to impress anyone, nor did he carry the weight of someone burdened by modern chaos. His face, framed by a graying beard, held the kind of stillness that only comes from prolonged solitude and introspection. There was something about him that made you feel like time itself slowed down in his presence. He didn't need to fill the silence with small talk. He was comfortable in stillness, in simplicity, in the space between words.

Scott was exactly the kind of person you'd expect to run a dark retreat—a guide into the void, someone who had likely sat in the darkness himself more times than he could count. He had the look of a wanderer who had stopped searching, a man who had already found what most people spend their whole lives chasing.

I gave Rod a big hug and thanked him for the ride. He gave me the proud look of a father—silent, steady, full of unspoken words. As he climbed back into his pickup truck, it hit me—there was no turning back now.

I climbed into Scott's ATV, and we started up the winding mountain path, the terrain growing rougher with each turn. The air was dry and crisp, carrying the sharp scent of pine. The roar of the engine shattered the silence, bouncing off the valley walls in a relentless echo—a stark contrast to the stillness of this place. The further we climbed, the more removed I felt from the outside world.

Eventually, we reached the top. Nestled into the rugged hillside were three small doors, built so seamlessly into the earth that they looked as though they had always been there. The nearest door was made of thick, honey-colored wood, its surface adorned with a small, flower-shaped window and a simple wooden latch. Framed by sturdy beams, it had the look of something ancient yet intentionally crafted.

The doors were set into a wall of stacked stones, each rock carefully placed, creating an organic blend with the landscape. Some stones were smooth and rounded, others jagged and raw, their earthy tones matching the dry, untamed terrain. Wild grasses and patches of dirt lined the ground, reinforcing the raw, off-grid feel of the place.

Inside the Retreat

Scott led me to the entrance and pulled open the heavy wooden door. A short staircase led down into a small entryway that felt like the opening to a hobbit home—cozy, earthy, and slightly surreal. The smell of burning sage filled my nose, instantly grounding me, reminding me of other transformative experiences I had embarked upon.

I had arrived earlier than most—11 a.m. instead of the usual check-in hours before sunset. Scott opened the second door leading to what looked like a bedroom. As I walked into the room, I stood in the dim light, taking in the space where I would spend the next four days in absolute darkness. The room was small yet inviting, a blend of rustic simplicity and intentional design. The walls were painted a deep, rich blue, grounding the space in a sense of stillness. Warm wooden trim framed the doors, adding a natural, earthy touch that softened the otherwise minimalist setting.

Across from the entrance, the bed was nestled into a custom wooden alcove, almost as if it had been carved directly into the wall. The sturdy frame extended seamlessly from the surrounding woodwork, enclosing the bed on three sides, creating a space that felt both protected and intentional—like a cocoon designed for deep rest. The mattress was covered in a simple, earth-toned blanket, its warm orange-brown hue blending effortlessly with the rich, natural wood.

A small built-in shelf extended from the headboard, just large enough to hold a cup of tea, a journal, or, in my case, nothing at all. The design was minimal, free of distractions, as if inviting me to surrender fully to the stillness. The entire structure felt like an anchor, grounding the space in a way that made it clear: This was not just a place to sleep—it was a place to retreat inward.

To the right of the bed, another small alcove opened up, designed for sitting, resting, or simply existing in stillness. A portable reclining chair sat tucked into the space, its sturdy frame and ergonomic design offering a rare touch of modern comfort in this otherwise simple, minimalist setting. Beside it, a meditation pillow rested on the floor, inviting a different kind of posture—one of presence, surrender, and deep contemplation.

Along the far wall, just before the entrance to the bathroom, a deep soaking tub sat nestled into the corner, its wooden paneling blending seamlessly with the room's rustic aesthetic. I didn't see it as just a place to bathe—it was one of the only things I could do in this room for the next four days. A bath wouldn't just be a way to clean myself. It would be a way to feel *something*—to break the monotony of the darkness, to experience warmth, weightlessness, and the sensation of water against my skin when everything else was swallowed by nothingness.

Beyond it, a narrow doorway led into the small bathroom. Inside, a simple toilet and sink stood against the wall, their presence a quiet luxury in an otherwise minimal space. There were no mirrors, no distractions—just the bare essentials, designed to serve without pulling focus from the journey inward.

Next to the front door, mounted against the wall, was a simple wooden box—an unassuming feature that would soon become my only connection to the outside world. This was where Scott would deliver my food once a day, placing it inside before shutting the door on his side. Only once it was fully closed could I open my side, ensuring that not even the faintest sliver of light would enter the room.

He explained that each delivery would contain enough food to last me twenty-four hours, but he wouldn't come at the same time every day. There would be no pattern, no sense of routine—only the quiet arrival of a meal in the darkness. Without clocks, without sunlight, without any external cues, I would have no way of knowing how much time had passed.

I would eat in total darkness, my hands feeling their way through each meal, my senses forced to adapt. This box, small and unremarkable, was the only tether to a world that was about to disappear.

Scott walked me through a final orientation, though there wasn't much to say. I would be in complete darkness with nothing to do—no distractions, no sense of time, just me and my mind. Afterward, he left me with two hours to settle in—to familiarize myself with my surroundings. I sat in the Adirondack chair outside the cave, book in hand, letting my eyes drift between the pages and the breathtaking expanse of mountains stretching before me. I knew this would be the last time I'd see anything for days, so I let myself take it all in—the vastness, the colors, the light—trying to imprint it in my mind before everything disappeared into darkness.

At exactly 1 p.m., Scott returned. His voice was steady, almost ceremonial.

"I'll come back once per day to deliver your food and check in. Other than that, you will be completely undisturbed until the end of your retreat."

Scott knelt by the door and showed me how to seal the final sliver of light, tucking a heavy blanket along the threshold. Then he left. I tucked the blanket back into place, and with that simple motion, the world disappeared.

Time Stretches

I lay on the bed, staring into nothing. Except *staring* wasn't the right word—there was nothing to stare at. Just blackness. Complete and total blackness. Nothing to see, nothing to do, nothing to distract me.

I shifted onto my side. Then onto my back. Still nothing. My mind searched for something to hold on to, something to do, but there was *nothing*.

I sat up, moved to the chair. Maybe sitting would feel different. It didn't. The same silence. The same void. The darkness pressed in on me —not just around me but inside me, filling every empty space where noise, color, and movement used to be.

I turned on the bath. The sound of water echoed in the small room, something *real* to latch on to. I sat on the edge, listening to it fill. Maybe this would be interesting. Maybe this would be something. But after a few minutes, the sound became just another version of silence.

I lowered myself into the tub, the warmth curling around me, offering a brief sensation of something *other* than the nothingness. I closed my eyes, but that didn't change anything. Eyes open or closed, it was the same.

After the bath, I moved to the meditation pillow, thinking, *This will help. This will give me purpose.* But meditation felt almost impossible. My mind kept reaching for reference points, for contrast, for *anything* that marked a difference between here and there, before and after. Normally, in meditation, closing your eyes signaled a shift, a transition inward. But here, there was no transition. No before or after. Just *this*.

And then, the obsession with time began.

How long had I been lying in bed? *Fifteen minutes?*

How long did I sit in the chair? *Maybe twenty?*

How long did it take the bath to fill? *Ten? Fifteen?*

How long did I sit in the tub? *Twenty?*

I started calculating, running mental math like a prisoner scratching tally marks into the walls of my mind. I guessed Scott would bring my food around 5 p.m. That was my next marker. My next *thing*.

That meant I had three more hours to go.

Three. More. Hours.

But it didn't feel like three hours. It felt like twelve. And that's when I realized—this wasn't going to be a four-day retreat. It was going to feel like fourteen.

What felt like an eternity later, I heard movement on the other side of the wall. Scott.

Finally.

Food. A distraction. Something to break the relentless monotony.

Through the wall, his muffled voice reached me—a welcome interruption to the crushing silence.

"How's it going?"

I hesitated. By my best guess, I had only been in the darkness for four hours. No way was I about to sound like a total wuss. Plus, Scott had gone out of his way to get me in at the last minute—I didn't want him thinking he had wasted the spot on someone who couldn't handle it.

"All good, man. Just settling in."

In reality, I was already suffering.

The darkness wasn't peaceful. It wasn't meditative. It was misery. Nothing to do. Nothing to distract my mind. And the more I thought about time, the slower it crawled. Every minute stretched, dragging endlessly into the next.

Just a few hours in, and it already felt like I had been here forever.

Lost in the Dark

I fumbled through the food Scott had left for me, relying entirely on touch. My fingers brushed against smooth plastic, then cool metal. I grabbed what felt like a thermos and twisted the lid. Lifting it to my nose, I inhaled—soup. But what kind? I took a cautious sip. Earthy, simple, like something made off the grid. The taste was unfamiliar, a mix of textures and flavors I couldn't quite place. *Maybe I'll save that for later.*

I reached into the box again, pulling out the next container. Hard edges, lightweight. I pried it open and ran my fingers across the contents —raw vegetables. Next. Another container. Something soft, giving slightly under my grip. A sandwich.

Please be good.

I peeled the bread apart slightly, running my thumb across the filling, trying to guess before I committed. Sticky. Smooth. Jackpot. PB&J on white bread.

I smiled to myself. A classic. A lifeline. Something familiar in a world that now felt completely foreign. I ate slowly, savoring every bite like it was my last connection to normalcy. When it was gone, I placed the remaining food back in the box, climbed into bed, and let the darkness swallow me again.

At some point, I drifted into sleep.

And then I dreamed.

I was still in the retreat. Still in the darkness. But in the dream, I couldn't take it anymore—I had to get out. I stumbled through the door into the night, gasping for freedom. Off in the distance, a highway. The glow of headlights cutting through the blackness. The hum of tires on pavement. Civilization.

A semi-truck pulled over, the driver rolling down the window.

"Need a ride?"

Relief flooded me. I climbed in, the warmth of the cab, the faint scent of diesel, the muffled radio in the background—every detail was comforting, a reminder that I was no longer alone.

He offered to take me to the nearest hotel. I had escaped.

But the moment I closed the truck door, I woke up.

Back to nothing.

The contrast was crippling. The joy I had felt in the dream—*the relief of being free*—was ripped away in an instant. The loneliness of the retreat came crashing down on me with twice the weight.

And the worst part? I had no idea if I had slept for eight hours or ten minutes.

I lay in bed, trapped in that hazy space between waking and dreaming, and all I could feel was time stretching endlessly ahead of me. My mind grasped for something solid, something to ground me in reality.

I reached out, feeling the soft texture of the blanket beneath my fingers. I listened, straining for any sound beyond the silence. Nothing. Just the steady rhythm of my own breath.

Why am I here, torturing myself?

The thought came instinctively, as if I had just woken up in an unfamiliar place. But I hadn't—I had chosen this.

But why?

Four days. No light. No sense of time.

This didn't feel like growth. It felt like self-harm.

And it felt familiar.

Running Toward Fear, Searching for Proof

I had thrown myself into experiences that pushed me to my edge, that stretched my mind to its absolute limits. The retreats. The sacred rituals. The indigenous initiations. The Hero's Journeys.

And not once did I stop to ask myself—*Should I do this?* Not once did I raise the white flag and scream SOS. It was as if I was trying to prove something at my own expense.

On the other side of these experiences, I always found clarity. A deeper understanding of myself. An expanded awareness. Another notch on my spiritual gangster belt.

But why was I drawn to experiences that would make most people run? Why was it that every time I heard about something that only a handful of people in the world had done—or would ever dare to do—a voice inside me whispered, "Do it?"

It wasn't that I wasn't afraid. I was terrified every time. But fear wasn't a stop sign—it was a summons. The moment something scared me, I had to do it. There was no other option.

I'd tell Brooks, "I just signed up for a retreat in the jungles of Costa Rica." She would give me that same perplexed look.

"Why?"

And my answer was always the same.

"Because I'm afraid to do it."

She would give me a concerned look and say, "That sounds like torture."

And it always was. Every time.

Brooks wasn't afraid of growth—far from it. She had walked her own path of challenges, of pushing past limitations. But she had an instinct for knowing the difference between something that stretched you and something that simply broke you.

I, on the other hand, ignored my instincts. I ran toward pain. I ran toward fear.

Every time that scared little boy inside me pleaded, *Don't do it,* another voice—The Man—shouted over him.

"Don't be a pussy. You have to do it. You have to prove that you're strong, that you're more capable and courageous than everyone else."

And I always listened.

I believed this was the only way. The only way to become the person I always wanted to be—strong, unwavering, fearless.

But lying on that bed, swallowed by complete darkness, I felt them both inside me at once.

The little boy, crying. The Man, controlling.

I felt their battle waging within me. I thought my session with Concetta had integrated them—merged them into me, brought them into harmony.

But now, in the silence, in the darkness, I realized—they were still fighting to be heard.

I had integrated them, yes—accepted their presence, acknowledged their voices.

But what I hadn't realized was that they weren't me.

They were echoes from the past, still trapped in the moments that created them. And every time I listened, every time I let them guide my decisions, I wasn't hearing the voice of the man I had become.

I was listening to two parts of me that had formed when I was just a child.

And even though I was in my late forties, I was still taking direction from voices that were forty years younger than me.

Voices that didn't belong in the present.

Voices that had no idea who I had become.

And in that moment, something shifted.

It was as if, in a matter of seconds, I grew up.

I saw the truth.

I didn't need to prove anything—to the world or to myself.

Because I already knew my worth. I already knew my strengths.

And my fears, my weaknesses?

They weren't failures. They weren't flaws. They weren't proof of my unworthiness.

They were what made me human.

They were what made me whole.

Letting Go

At that moment, I made a decision. I was done torturing myself. I would leave the darkness.

And the second I made that choice, something shifted. The weight of the void, the suffocating stillness—it all felt just a little lighter. The darkness was still there, pressing in from every direction, but now, it wasn't all there was.

My mind drifted to gratitude—to Brooks, my kids, my parents, my siblings. To my experience at Tagger, to every hard-earned lesson that had led me here.

And for the first time in my life, I let myself feel immense gratitude for myself.

I thought about everything I had built, learned, endured. The love I had given. The honesty and integrity I had lived by. The high standards I set for myself. My work ethic, my discipline, my ability to commit to something and see it through, no matter how difficult.

Even my flaws—the mistakes, the missteps, the moments that once made me cringe—I felt gratitude for them too. They had shaped me just as much as my successes.

And then it hit me.

I had spent my entire life trying to prove something—that I was strong enough, disciplined enough, fearless enough. That I could become the kind of man I had always looked up to—my father, my grandfather.

But in that moment of stillness, I realized—I didn't need to become anything.

I was simply content being myself.

Redefining Strength

Later that day, when Scott came to deliver my food, I told him I was leaving the cave. I'd stay one more night, but I asked him to come back the next day at 11 a.m. to get me. I braced myself for resistance—for him to challenge my decision, to tell me I just needed to push through, that the real transformation was waiting on the other side of my discomfort.

But he didn't.

He simply said, "I'll see you tomorrow," as if he understood what had just happened.

This was the first time I had ever walked away from something unfinished. And yet quitting didn't feel like failure. I had spent my entire life believing transformation meant fighting, enduring, pushing through resistance at all costs. But this was different. This wasn't about breaking myself down just to prove I could survive it. This was about finding myself. Choosing for myself. Reclaiming my agency.

And I think Scott knew that.

He understood that the amount of time spent in the darkness wasn't the point. The point was what I found while I was there—and more importantly, what I was choosing for myself when I decided to leave.

I wasn't proving my strength by pushing through. I was proving it by knowing when to walk away.

On the threshold, moments before stepping into the cave—and into myself.

This is what the inside of the cave looked like—right before the lights went out.

16

EVOLVEWELL

"The breath is the bridge which connects life to consciousness, which unites your body to your thoughts."
—Thích Nhất Hạnh

When I returned from Oregon, I had clarity—not just about who I was but about what I wanted to create.

The darkness had stripped everything away. The noise, the distractions, the need to prove something. All that remained was the truth.

I felt lighter, and the relentless pressure to chase, to push, to force things into existence was gone—like a storm that had finally passed, leaving only clear skies in its wake. Instead, I felt aligned—as if everything I had experienced up until now had been leading me to this exact moment.

For years, I had immersed myself in personal transformation. I had walked through fire—literally and figuratively—seeking growth, testing my limits, expanding my awareness. And while each experience had changed me, none of them had ever fully answered the deeper question: What was my true purpose?

Ikigai—The Intersection of Purpose

I had spent my life chasing growth, pushing myself into discomfort, and testing my limits in search of something I couldn't quite name. But after emerging from the darkness, I finally had the space to ask the right question: *Why am I here?*

That's when I thought about a term Rod often spoke about— *Ikigai.*

A Japanese concept that loosely translates to "reason for being," *Ikigai* is the place where passion, mission, vocation, and profession intersect—where what you love, what you're good at, what the world needs, and what you can be paid for all align.

For so long, I had excelled at building things. Businesses. Teams. Ideas. But I had never stopped to ask myself if what I was building truly aligned with my *Ikigai.*

Was I simply creating because it would give me the success I had always dreamed about? Because it felt safe? Because it was another challenge to conquer?

Yes, I had achieved success, but had I been fulfilling my purpose?

Ikigai isn't just about passion—it's about meaning. It's about waking up each day with a sense of direction, knowing that what you do matters not just to you but to the world. And for the first time, I saw exactly where my *Ikigai* lived.

It wasn't just about building another company—it had to mean something.

For years, I had created, scaled, and led businesses. I knew how to build. I knew how to grow. But this time, it wasn't about revenue models, market trends, or chasing the next big thing.

It was about impact.

It was about building something that truly mattered—something that had the power to change lives.

I knew then that whatever I created next had to be a direct expression of who I was and what I valued. It couldn't just be another project

—it had to be a culmination of everything I had learned, everything I had experienced, and everything I had become. It needed to blend my passion for transformation, my years of experience in technology, and my desire to help others grow. It had to be something that didn't just challenge me but elevated the people around me.

Something that didn't just exist for success—but for meaning.

I had already made enough money. I had already achieved success. The things I once chased—the financial security, the recognition, the external validation—were no longer the driving force.

This time, I wasn't building for the sake of winning. I was building for the sake of creating something real, something that mattered.

And with that clarity, I picked up the phone and called Rod.

"Let's do it. Let's start this company."

The Birth of EvolveWell

The first thing Rod did was introduce me to his business partner, Alex King-Harris—a man unlike anyone I had ever met.

Alex and Rod first crossed paths years earlier when Alex moved to Ashland, Oregon. There, they co-created a rites of passage and mentorship program for struggling teens, guiding young men through pivotal life transitions. Eventually, their paths diverged, but as often happens when something is meant to be, the universe brought them back together at exactly the right time.

By then, Alex had been developing a neural reprogramming system that combined contemporary research in neuroscience, spirituality, and personal growth to help people break free from limiting patterns and create lasting change. A deep dive into AI had expanded his vision, opening up new possibilities for how his system could evolve. Around that same time, Rod caught wind of what Alex was working on, and after reconnecting, Alex introduced him to AI.

Rod immediately saw the potential—specifically in using AI for journaling. The idea sparked something in him, and he quickly began experimenting with ChatGPT, using it to enhance self-reflection and personal growth. That's when he pitched Alex on building an AI-driven journaling app.

At first, Alex resisted. Like me, he had already been through the grind of launching a startup and wasn't eager to step into that world again. But Rod was relentless, convinced that together they could create something groundbreaking. After plenty of conversations—and some persistent convincing—Alex finally agreed.

Everything was aligning. Their work had prepared me for my own transformation, and in turn, my experience in the darkness gave me absolute clarity—this was exactly what I wanted to build, but on an even bigger scale.

My experience at Tagger, building a B2B platform and scaling it globally, had given me the perspective to see how Rod and Alex's vision could be expanded into something even more far-reaching. What they had created was already profound, but I saw an opportunity to build on it—to develop a platform that could not only transform individuals but also empower coaches and therapists.

By providing professionals with tools to support their clients between sessions, track progress, and reinforce transformation, we could bridge the gap between personal growth and professional guidance.

Their foundation was strong. Together, we could take it to the world.

And with that, EvolveWell was born.

The Rare Bird

Alex has one of those rare minds—he's a sharp business strategist with the talent of an artist. Moving effortlessly between worlds, he's equally at home discussing market dynamics and composing music that stirs the soul.

A formally trained jazz and classical musician, Alex is one of the most talented artists I have ever known. Under the name Rara Avis (Latin for 'rare bird'), he has co-created globally acclaimed music projects like Desert Dwellers, Shamans Dream, and Liquid Bloom, beautifully crafting sonic landscapes designed to enhance breathwork, movement, and deep transformation. His music is more than just something you listen to—it's something you *feel*, something that moves through you.

But Alex isn't just an artist—he's also an entrepreneur.

As Co-Founder and CEO of YogiTunes—a streaming platform built specifically for the wellness space—Alex had been through the grind of a startup, just like I had. He knew what it meant to build something from the ground up—to sacrifice everything to bring a vision to life.

What struck me even more than his entrepreneurial experience was his devotion to transformation. He had spent years mentoring youth, guiding men through rites of passage, and supporting people in addiction recovery.

When Rod introduced me to Alex, I knew immediately—this was someone I wanted to work with, someone I could learn from.

And together, we were about to build something entirely new—a company that would stretch my understanding of what a business could be, what it could do, and how it should operate.

The Breath That Changed Everything

Building this company wasn't just about strategy and execution—it was about embodying the very transformation we wanted to create for others. And Alex lived and breathed that transformation in a way I had never seen before.

The day after I met Alex, he looked at me and said, "You've got to try this."

He had been talking to me about breathwork, explaining how it could shift my entire state of being, but I was skeptical. I had done breathwork before, and it always felt forced—like an intense workout at the gym rather than a path to transformation.

But Alex approached it differently. Instead of just telling me to do it, he explained why it worked—what was happening in my body, my brain, my nervous system. And I was fascinated by the science.

"Breath is the only part of your autonomic nervous system that you can control," he said. "You can't consciously slow your digestion or adjust your heart rate at will. But your breath? That's the bridge between your conscious and unconscious self."

He went on to explain that when you change your breathing, you change your state—physically, mentally, emotionally.

Slow, deep breathing activates the parasympathetic nervous system, shifting the body into rest-and-digest mode, lowering stress hormones, and creating a sense of calm. Fast, intense breathwork can do the opposite—flooding the body with oxygen, stimulating the sympathetic nervous system, and triggering heightened states of awareness.

"Most people don't realize it, but the way you breathe shapes your entire experience of life," Alex said. "Your breath patterns influence your stress levels, your focus, your emotions—most importantly, even your thoughts."

I had always seen breathwork as an effort, something I had to force myself through. But for Alex, it wasn't about effort—it was about allowing breath to guide you into a different state of being. To tap into an intelligence inside your body that is waiting to be discovered.

And I was curious.

"Alright," I said. "Let's do it."

Learning to Breathe

Over the next two weeks, Alex taught me the fundamentals of breathwork—not as a chore or a practice to get through but as a tool to shape my entire state of being.

I had always thought of breathing as automatic, something my body did on its own. But Alex showed me that breath is the one unconscious function we can control—and by controlling it, we can control everything else.

We started with slow, steady breaths, the kind that instantly calmed my nervous system. "This brings you into coherence," Alex explained. "Heart rate, brainwaves, emotions—everything starts to synchronize when you breathe like this." I could feel it immediately. My body softened, my thoughts slowed, and for the first time in a while, I felt completely present.

Then he had me hold my breath after an exhale. At first, my body panicked—lungs screaming for air, begging to inhale—but I held on, waiting. When I finally inhaled again, a wave of warmth spread through my chest.

"That's your body releasing adrenaline," Alex said. "You're rewiring your stress response."

Some days, he had me breathe fast and deep, pulling in huge gulps of air, then exhaling in sharp bursts. Within minutes, I felt lightheaded, almost euphoric, like I had tapped into some hidden energy source I never knew existed. Other times, the breath was slow, controlled—expanding my belly, filling my lungs completely before releasing in a long, deliberate exhale.

"This is how you shift your state," Alex told me. "You can wake yourself up, you can slow yourself down, you can access deeper parts of your mind—all with breath."

By the end of the first week, he had me doing something that felt impossible—breathing out all my air after a round of breathwork and holding my breath with empty lungs for two and a half minutes.

At first, my body fought it—my chest tightening, my brain screaming for air. But Alex's voice kept me steady.

"Just relax. The panic is just your mind reacting. Let it pass."

So I waited.

At thirty seconds, my body tensed. At a minute, my instincts told me to inhale. But then something strange happened—I settled in. The desperation faded, and my body simply *stopped fighting*.

Two minutes.

Two and a half.

When I finally took a slow, measured breath in, I felt a rush of energy move through me—like I had just tapped into something deeper, something I didn't know I was capable of.

I looked at Alex, stunned.

"Told you," he said with a grin.

I had never thought of breath as a lever I could pull, something that could make me calm, alert, clear, or even expansive. And for the first time, breathwork didn't feel like effort. It felt like freedom.

I had spent so much of my life trying to force transformation—pushing myself to extremes, chasing discomfort, proving I could endure.

But here was something simple, something always available, something that didn't require suffering.

Just breath.

And that changed everything.

It felt like the universe had placed Alex in my life at exactly the right time—to deepen my understanding of what my body was truly capable of. His presence cracked something open in me and reinforced what I had learned, time and time again: Transformation doesn't just happen in solitude.

It happens in relationship.

It happens in community.

And if you're open—*truly open*—the universe will introduce you to people who will impact your life in the most surprising and profound ways—always arriving right on time.

Alex was one of those people.

And so was Vuk Baletic.

When the Right People Show Up

Vuk (pronounced "Vook") was one of our first employees at Tagger.

A towering 6'9" Serbian, he had the analytical mind of a strategist and the heart of an adventurer. Originally from Belgrade, Vuk started at Tagger in our Los Angeles office, quickly proving himself invaluable—not just because of his ability to break down complex customer problems but because he could see the vision through the noise of customer requests.

Unlike many, Vuk didn't just do his job—he anticipated where the company needed to go. He started in customer success but later transitioned into product development and sales, bridging the gap between what clients wanted and what we were building. Fluent in English, Serbian, and Spanish, he could be on a call with a client in London one moment, then seamlessly switch to Spanish for a client in Mexico moments later. His ability to connect with people, no matter their background, made him a force.

Vuk and I traveled together often, particularly to Kraków for development meetings. Over the years, our relationship evolved from employer-employee to something much deeper—a friendship rooted in mutual respect, shared adventures, and a relentless pursuit of growth. We had our fair share of fun too. In Kraków, we'd walk through the crowded streets at night, passing by open-air restaurants filled with people drinking and laughing. Without fail, as we passed, conversations at every table would pause as heads turned—especially the women—just to get a look at the giant man walking beside me. I had never felt so insignificant, and it made me laugh every time.

Like me, Vuk had his own personal growth path—whether it was heading into the jungle for a spiritual retreat or climbing snowy mountains in nothing but shorts to complete his Wim Hof training. We constantly inspired each other, swapping stories of transformation, pushing each other toward the next level.

He left Tagger just before the sale to pursue his passion for helping others transform their lives, a decision I supported 100 percent. But as I would soon learn, our paths would cross again in the most unexpected way.

The Universe Has Its Own Timing

Once I decided to start EvolveWell with Rod and Alex, we took a retreat to map out the future of the company. On the first night, we laid everything out—what the platform needed, the essential features, the big picture vision.

But one crucial piece was still unresolved.

We had the vision, but how were we actually going to build this?

I knew enough developers to piece together a tech team, but that wasn't as easy as it sounded. You don't just need coders—you need a team with the right expertise, alignment, and ability to bring a vision like EvolveWell to life. The platform had to be built by people who understood both technology and transformation, who could execute at the highest level and adapt as we evolved.

I went to bed that night excited for the future, but that question— How are we going to build this?—lingered.

I had promised myself I wouldn't force things anymore. That I'd let life unfold as it needed to, without trying to strong-arm my way to success. And sure enough, the universe stepped in.

The next morning, I woke up, checked my phone, and saw a WhatsApp message from Vuk:

"Hey Pete, hope you're having a great weekend. I heard about the new company you're building, and I think we should build a dev team in Serbia."

I stared at the screen and laughed.

Of course, Vuk had sent this message at the exact right moment, without even knowing I'd spent the night wondering how to solve this exact problem.

I didn't overthink it. I didn't analyze it. I just texted back:

"Perfect timing. Let's fucking go!"

We had the vision. Now we had the team to bring it to life.

Personal Growth Before Profits

EvolveWell isn't simply about building a platform—it's about building a new way of doing business. From the beginning, we knew we weren't here to create just another tech company. We were here to create a company that puts people before profits, one where personal growth is built into the very DNA of how we operate.

It's not only about offering tools for transformation—we're committed to living the work. Our employees aren't here only to build a product—they're here to grow. We made a decision early on—to invest in the personal development of our team the same way we invest in the business itself.

That's why we pay our employees to go on transformative experiences, like Dr. Joe Dispenza retreats, where they can deepen their awareness, expand their consciousness, and unlock their full potential. These aren't just company perks—they're experiences designed to help our team become more aligned, present, and fulfilled, both in their work and in their personal lives.

Three days a week, we shut everything down for a one-hour breathwork and meditation session called *Jams*, led by Alex. It's not just about stress relief or improving focus—it's about creating a workplace where people actually feel better. A place where they don't have to sacrifice themselves to be successful.

We're proving that business can be done differently. That success doesn't have to come at the cost of well-being. That investing in employees' transformation isn't just good for them—it's good for the company too.

A Space for Deep Connection

In addition to *Jams*, we have team check-ins twice a week—but these aren't the usual surface-level meetings about deadlines or project updates. They go deeper. They're more human.

These check-ins are sacred spaces where employees are truly invited to bring their whole selves. People share their proudest achievements, not just at work but in their personal lives. They speak about breakthroughs, the moments they change their patterns, the challenges they overcome.

And just as importantly, they share their struggles—the things weighing on them, the doubts creeping in, the fears they're working through. There's no expectation to perform, no pressure to put on a brave face. Just honesty. Just presence.

And then—silence.

No one jumps in with advice. No one follows up with a "Here's what worked for me." No one tries to fix, soften, or reframe anything.

Because that's not the point.

The point is simply to let it out—to be witnessed by another human being and let it hang there, unpolished, unfiltered, unresolved. To be heard, without needing a solution.

Over time, these check-ins become more than just a space to speak—they become a mirror.

When someone shares their story, you can't help but see yourself in it. The details might be different, but the core experience—the struggle, the doubt, the learning—is always the same.

Hearing someone wrestle with imposter syndrome makes you

confront the ways you still question your own worth. Listening to someone describe a painful setback reminds you of the times you've been knocked down and forced to rebuild. Even the triumphs—the moments of growth, of courage, of breaking through old patterns—become reminders of what's possible in your own life.

Week after week, these sessions reflect back your own work, your own blind spots, your own journey.

Because transformation doesn't just happen in isolation—it happens in relationship. When you see your own life lessons woven into someone else's story, when their breakthroughs awaken something dormant in you, when their courage gives you permission to step more fully into your own.

Breathing New Life into Business

EvolveWell isn't just about doing great work—it's about becoming the kind of people who can sustain that work without burning out, shutting down, or losing ourselves in the process.

Because when people feel seen, supported, and aligned, they don't only work harder—they work better. They create better. They live better.

And we aren't just doing this for ourselves. We're creating a space for coaches and therapists, friends and family to join in our practice. A place where people can come to do the work, to grow, to expand—just as we are.

Twice a week, we offer these sessions to our growing community, giving people the opportunity to connect, reflect, and engage in the same breathwork and meditation practices that have transformed our own lives.

To help others find fulfillment, purpose, and transformation in their own lives.

To create a community of individuals committed to their own evolution—not just in their careers but in how they live, love, and show up for themselves every single day.

And in doing so, sure, we're trying to make an impact in the coaching world and in the tech world—but more importantly, we're transforming the way people live, work, and connect with themselves and each other.

One breath at a time.

17

BECOMING THE PRACTICE

"Be the change that you wish to see in the world."
—Mahatma Gandhi

E verything changed when I stopped chasing transformation and started practicing it.

I developed a daily practice of breathwork and meditation that continues to shape everything I do. More than a routine, this practice has become a tool for navigating life with presence and intention. When I engage in breathwork and meditation, I'm consciously cultivating elevated emotional states—shaping my health, sharpening my clarity, and strengthening my ability to show up fully. Instead of waking up and immediately succumbing to stress, I've learned to tune into my inner compass, letting it guide me toward peace, clarity, and joy.

My Practice

Lasting transformation doesn't happen in a single breakthrough—it happens through repetition. It happens when you return to the same practice, day after day, and get quiet enough to reconnect with who you are beneath the noise, beneath your patterns, and beneath the roles you've learned to play.

My daily practice begins with breathwork.

It's my gateway—shifting me from a state of doing to a state of being. Each inhale is an invitation to return to the present moment. Each exhale is a release of what no longer serves me. With each breath, I give my body permission to soften, unwind, and open. And the more I breathe, the more my unconscious thoughts dissolve, and the million things on my to-do list simply drift away.

In that grounded place, breathwork has done its job—cleared the mind, opened the channels, and brought me home to myself. That's where coherence returns—my systems shift from survival to harmony, from fragmentation to flow. My heart opens, sending signals of peace and order to my brain. I become less mechanical, more intuitive. Less reactive, more creative.

And once I arrive in that space of inner stillness and balance, I move into meditation to consciously cultivate the thoughts and emotions I want to carry into my day—elevated states like joy, gratitude, and love. I'm not waiting for something outside of me to spark those feelings—I'm choosing to feel them now. And I do that intentionally, by calling those emotions into my body.

If I want to cultivate more love in my life, I think about my wife and my children. I picture their faces and feel the unconditional bond that connects us. I reflect on the depth of my devotion—the instinct to protect them, to care for them, to stand beside them no matter what. I don't just think about love—I become it. I let it radiate from my heart and flood my entire body.

If I want to cultivate more gratitude in my life, I think about the journey that brought me here—the wild, winding path filled with breakdowns, breakthroughs, detours, and divine interventions. I feel the weight of that journey in my chest and a deep appreciation for the life I get to live today. I don't just think about gratitude—I become it. I let it expand from my heart and flood my entire body.

If I want to cultivate more joy in my life, I think about being in service to others and supporting their growth. I think about the moments when someone remembers who they truly are—when the light comes back on. I feel the power of their transformation and the privilege of witnessing it unfold. I don't just think about joy—I become it. I let it rise from my heart and flood my entire body.

The more I practice cultivating these emotions during meditation, the more familiar they become. Over time, they begin to shape how I think, how I move, and how I connect. They become my emotional foundation.

That's the shift. That's the moment—when my elevated thoughts and emotions stop being the exception and start becoming the norm.

Finding Your Path

I used to believe transformation had to be earned through suffering.

So I pushed myself to the edge of discomfort—again and again—believing that the more pain I endured, the more enlightened I'd become.

And while those experiences shaped me, they also taught me something important:

Growth doesn't have to be so hard. Transformation can be simple.

Simple—but not effortless.

Transformation doesn't require suffering, but it does require commitment. It's not about how much you endure. It's about how consistently you show up for yourself.

Rod taught me that real transformation demands full commitment. It doesn't happen by accident. It doesn't happen by dabbling. It requires structure, discipline, and a willingness to surrender to the process. The people who change—the ones who truly break through—are the ones who show up, every day, and do the work.

All you need to do is find what works for you.

Start by exploring—go on YouTube, Google, or any platform, and search for breathwork and meditation videos. Try different styles. Play with different rhythms. See what resonates.

There's no single breathwork that's "the most transformative," no one meditation that's "the best." It's not about perfection—it's about connection. It's about finding the practice that brings you back to yourself.

And if breathwork or meditation don't resonate right away, explore other modalities.

Try Qigong, journaling, yoga, chanting, or cold plunges.

The point isn't *what* you do. The point is that you *do*.

What matters most is that you show up. Stay curious. Keep listening for what feels right—for your body, your rhythm, your life.

And if you're not sure where to begin, start here.

Start Here

I've put together a series of breathwork and meditation videos designed to help you drop in, reset, and reconnect with yourself. This is the same practice I return to each morning to anchor into stillness, clarity, and purpose—to shift from doing to being, from chaos to coherence, from distraction to deep presence.

This isn't about fixing yourself; it's about coming home to yourself.

Each session is an invitation to meet yourself where you are, without judgment or expectation. Whether you're brand new to this kind of work or returning after time away, this practice is here to gently guide you back—back to your breath, your body, your truth.

There's no pressure to complete a challenge or follow a strict routine, just a simple invitation to slow down, breathe, and remember the version of you that already holds the clarity, peace, and presence you seek.

Let these videos be a doorway—a doorway into yourself, into a quieter mind, a calmer nervous system, a fuller heart. Return to them as often as you need; allow them to support *your* journey of remembering.

You can access all the videos for free at www.EvolveWeird.com.

And yes, it's *Evolve Weird*, because transformation never unfolds the way we think it will. It's messy, mysterious, and full of surprises. The experiences that truly transform us are usually the ones we never saw coming.

If you'd like to connect with others walking this path, I invite you to join our weekly EvolveWell Breathwork and Meditation Jams. No cost. No experience needed. Just a desire to evolve.

You can find dates and times at www.EvolveWell.com/Jams.

18

THE CHOICE

"When we strive to become better than we are, everything around us becomes better too."
—Paulo Coelho

In June 2024, Brooks and I traveled to Cancun, Mexico, for a week-long advanced retreat with Dr. Joe Dispenza. Alongside 1,500 other attendees, we embarked on a journey of deep meditation, profound learning, and personal transformation.

I had heard that at some point during the retreat, we would do a five-hour meditation starting at 4 a.m. It sounded horrible—but that was exactly why I wanted to do it. I knew it would push me beyond my comfort zone. And beyond my comfort zone was where transformation lived.

But despite knowing better, I walked into that meditation wanting an outcome. I had taken a week out of my life and flown down to Mexico, and I wanted something to happen. A breakthrough. A vision. A shift. And how do you guarantee an outcome? With force and control. If you ever want to experience pain and suffering, try controlling the outcome of a five-hour meditation.

The first three hours were pure torture. My body ached. My mind fought it every step of the way. I wanted a revelation, a truth, a transformation. And the more I wanted those things, the further they drifted away.

Remember the paradox of seeking? The moment we declare that we want something, we reinforce the belief that we lack it. The more we chase something, the further we push it away. And once again, I found myself chasing. Trying to control the experience. Trying to control the outcome.

But transformation doesn't come from control. It comes from surrender. And you can surrender the easy way or the hard way. The easy way was never my way.

Standing Before Source

Three hours in, I finally hit my breaking point. Just like in the temazcal, I had reached the edge of my own suffering. I was lost. Drowning in resistance. But then—something extraordinary happened.

One moment, I was in a room with 1,500 people. The next, I was somewhere else entirely. Where I was, I didn't know. But I found myself standing in front of Source. The Source of everything.

Her presence was undeniable. Infinite. Loving. Unimaginably vast. And yet, despite her enormity, I felt small in the best way possible—like a child in the presence of something so much greater than myself. So, instinctively, I did what a child would do.

I asked all the questions I had spent a lifetime searching for.
What is consciousness?
What is oneness?
Why am I here?
I called her Mother, and she called me Child.

And suddenly, I felt it—the innocence, the smallness, the sheer awe of being in the presence of something so vast. Not a child being judged. A child being loved. A child being guided by wisdom beyond my comprehension.

And then, through the overwhelming love, a question rose within me—one I had never considered before.

"Mother, what happened when my grandfather died?"

She responded gently but without hesitation. "Child, I will show you."

And suddenly, I saw him. Not just a memory, not just an image—I was witnessing his journey. There he stood, in front of Source, his spirit radiating a quiet pride—the pride of a life well lived and the contributions he left behind. He was content. At peace.

And then, with the kind of courage I had only seen once before—that same unbreakable knowing in the eyes of the Native American in the temazcal—he stepped into oneness. No hesitation. No fear. No resistance. Just knowing.

The Cost of Awakening

I swallowed hard. I was in awe of this man—his courage, his wisdom, his unwavering trust. For a moment, I felt that same immense peace my grandfather had stepped into, and bliss filled every cell of my body.

Then a thought surfaced.

"Mother, why don't we all feel this happiness all the time? Why is there so much pain and suffering in this world?"

She answered as if she had been waiting for this question all along.

"Child, in order to know joy and happiness, you must know pain and sadness. Without one, you cannot experience the other. Would you like to feel the sadness of the world?"

I hesitated for only a moment before whispering, "Yes, Mother."

And in an instant, it was like she tapped me on the head with a magic wand. I was overwhelmed by all the grief and suffering in the world. It slammed into me like a tidal wave. Tears poured down my face. My chest heaved with sobs. It wasn't just my pain—I felt all of it. The sorrow of every grieving mother. The loneliness of every abandoned child. The suffering of every soul that had ever known heartbreak, war, loss, despair.

It was too much.

And then—amid the suffocating sadness—I felt it. A hand on my back. Warm, grounding, loving. Brooks. A reminder that I'm not alone. That even in the depth of suffering, there is love. Another tender act from our sacred agreement.

At some point, I couldn't take it anymore. "Please, Mother, make it stop." And just like that—it stopped. The weight lifted. My tears slowed. I sat there, exhausted.

Then, her voice again. "Child, would you now like to feel joy, love, and happiness?"

I barely got the words out. "Yes, please, Mother."

And again—as if with a single touch—everything changed. Suddenly, I was flooded with love. Not just warmth. Not just happiness. Pure, uncontainable, infinite love. Love for myself. Love for Brooks. Love for my kids, my parents, my siblings. Love for every single person in that room. And it kept expanding. Love for my city. Love for my country. Love for every single human on Earth. Until my love encircled the entire world.

And just like that—it was over. I was back in the room. Brooks still holding me.

And in that moment, I understood.

The Truth

We are here to live it. To feel it. *All of it.*

The love. The sadness. The joy. The pain. The pure exhilaration of achieving something you never thought possible.

Not to chase. Not to conquer. Not to escape or transcend this human experience.

Because the only way to truly experience life is to surrender to all it has to offer.

You are here to experience it all—the joy, the pain, the heartbreak, the triumph. To live, not just exist.

And when you allow yourself to surrender to the discomfort of being human—when you strip away all the distractions, all the ways we numb ourselves—you're left with one undeniable truth: *Being human is hard.*

But this life—the one you're living—is the life your soul chose. It wanted the challenge. The uncertainty. The breakthroughs. The love. The loss.

Your soul chose to be human because it's the hardest path to growth —but also the fastest.

And only the most fearless, relentless, badass souls choose to be human. Because they know—this is where the real work happens.

It's all part of the deal. Your soul didn't come here to play it safe. It came here to grow and experience it all.

So why would you sit on the sidelines, numbing yourself, watching life pass you by? Why would you settle for anything less than your fullest potential?

You are here to experience it all.

What's stopping you?

Taking Inventory

It's time to take an *honest* inventory of your life.

Am I truly fulfilled, or just comfortable?

When was the last time I felt fully alive—not just going through the motions but deeply connected to what I'm doing and why?

Do I fully love myself, or do I only love the version of me that's successful, productive, or making others happy?

What would change if I treated myself with the same love and compassion I so freely give to others?

Am I chasing goals that fulfill me, or just ones I believe will finally make me *enough*?

Where am I outsourcing my worth—seeking validation, approval, or permission to be who I already know I am?

What parts of me have I abandoned to fit in, to feel accepted, to feel safe?

And the biggest question of all: if I fully loved and trusted myself, how would my life be different?

Because in the end, it all comes down to this: not just success, not just discipline, but radical self-love.

The kind that makes you stop settling. The kind that demands more. The kind that refuses to wait another damn day to start truly living.

That's when life cracks open.

That's when you start listening—really listening—to the voice that's been there all along. The one gently guiding you back home to yourself.

That's when you realize—you were never lost. You were just too busy pushing, forcing, gripping so tightly that you couldn't hear the call.

Because real transformation doesn't come from control. It comes from surrender.

And that kind of surrender? It requires a complete mind erase.

Imagine, just for a moment, that you forgot everything. Your past. Your definition of happiness. Your concept of success. Your deepest beliefs about who you are.

All of it.

No childhood conditioning. No inherited ideas about what it means to be good, successful, or worthy. No expectations from society, family, or friends shaping your choices.

No stories from your past holding you back.

It's just you—a blank slate.

If there were no expectations—no fear of failure, no rules telling you what's possible or impossible—what kind of life would you create?

Would you chase the same things? Would you still measure your worth by productivity, achievement, external validation?

Would you still carry the same doubts, the same limitations, the same fear of not being enough?

Or would you build something entirely different?

Would you allow yourself to choose joy over obligation, love over scarcity, purpose over approval?

Would you trust yourself—fully and completely—without needing permission from anyone else?

Because here's the truth—and this might blow your mind:

You get to choose.

Your Time Is Now

You lucky son of a gun—this is *your* life.

And for some reason, beyond logic, beyond understanding, you were chosen to be here.

Just think about that—out of all the possibilities, out of all the odds stacked against you, you won the ultimate golden lottery.

The odds of you existing? Practically zero. About 1 in 400 trillion.

And yet—here you are.

So the real question is—will you embrace this miracle and live it fully, or will you let it slip by, waiting for a "someday" that never comes?

Stop waiting. Stop hesitating. Stop bargaining with your own potential.

This is your life. No one is going to hand you the perfect moment, the perfect plan, the perfect version of yourself.

You either go all in or you don't.

You either step into the fire—into the discomfort, the risk, the unknown—or you sit back, watch the days pass, and wonder what could have been.

So stand the fuck up. Take this life by the balls. And go after what sets your soul on fire.

Fail loudly. Love recklessly. Live fully.

Because this is it.

This is your time.

This is why you're here:

To remember who you've always been.

And I can't wait to see you fully step into that truth.

AFTERWORD

I knew I wanted to tell my story—but I also knew I'd need help shaping it. Not because I didn't have something to say, but because I wanted to say it clearly, truthfully, and with the depth it deserved.

I didn't want a ghostwriter. I didn't want someone to shape my story for me. I wanted to do the work—every sentence, every insight, every raw moment—because this isn't just a book about transformation.

It's part of the transformation.

Still, I needed support. I needed a mirror, a sounding board, a creative partner—something that could help me clarify what I was trying to say without diluting the voice I had spent years learning to trust.

So I did something a little unconventional.

I worked with AI.

Not to replace my voice—but to sharpen it. To hold space for it. I wrote. I revised. I wrestled with the words. And AI became part of that process. Not the author. Not the message. But a strange and surprisingly helpful tool that helped me tell my story in the truest way I could.

Some people might judge that. I'm okay with it.

Because if *The Remembering* taught me anything, it's that growth never shows up the way we expect it to. It's not linear. It's not neat. It's not always comfortable. It's often weird, often beautiful—and rarely what we expect.

Yes, AI played a role in bringing this book to life.

But this is not a book about technology.

It's about the raw, unpredictable, deeply human process of remembering who you really are.

Because in the end, growth isn't about the tools we use—it's about our willingness to evolve, no matter how weird our journey may be.

ABOUT THE AUTHOR

Peter Kennedy is an entrepreneur and seeker of transformation. As the founder of multiple companies, he has spent his career at the intersection of business, technology, and personal growth. From launching and scaling startups to leading a company through acquisition by a publicly traded company, Peter has experienced firsthand the highs and lows of entrepreneurship—the relentless drive, the sacrifices, and ultimately, the realization that success alone doesn't lead to fulfillment.

After years of chasing external achievements, he discovered that real transformation isn't about reaching the next milestone—it's about evolving with intention, purpose, and authenticity. This realization led him to co-create EvolveWell, Inc., an AI-powered platform designed to help coaches and therapists support their clients between sessions, bridging the gap between structured guidance and real-life change.

In *The Remembering*, Peter shares his unconventional path, the lessons learned through discomfort and breakthroughs, and a new way of approaching life—one rooted in vision and alignment with the universe. Through raw storytelling and deep insights, he invites readers to rethink growth, embrace the unexpected, and step boldly into the unknown.

Peter lives in Los Angeles with his wife and five children.